Widening the Horizons

Widening the Horizons
Pastoral Responses to a Fragmented Society

Charles V. Gerkin

The Westminster Press
Philadelphia

Scripture quotations from the Revised Standard Version of the Bible are copyrighted 1946, 1952, ©1971, 1973 by the Division of Christian Education of the National Council of the Churches of Christ in the U.S.A. and are used by permission.

Book design by Gene Harris

First edition

Published by The Westminster Press®
Philadelphia, Pennsylvania

PRINTED IN THE UNITED STATES OF AMERICA

9 8 7 6 5 4 3 2 1

Library of Congress Cataloging-in-Publication Data

Gerkin, Charles V., 1922–
  Widening the horizons.

  Bibliography: p.
  Includes index.
  1. Pastoral theology. 2. Theology, Practical.
I. Title.
BV4011.G46 1986   253   86-7832
  ISBN 0-664-24037-2 (pbk.)

In memory of
TOM and JOE
my spiritual brothers

Thomas W. Klink
1920–1970

Joseph E. Caldwell
1918–1967

Contents

Acknowledgments

It is impossible to undertake the writing of a book without support from others of several kinds. Institutions and grant-giving agencies must provide the institutional and financial support to make the work possible. Professional friends and colleagues must be available to give both encouragement and criticism at numerous points along the way. Families need to be understanding about inordinate preoccupations that possess the writer concerning ideas and problems that often seem esoteric and obscure. One does not write a book solely on one's own.

I have been most fortunate in the writing of this book to have had support at all these levels. Emory University provided the sabbatical year during which much of the work was accomplished and, in addition, provided a generous grant through the Emory University Research Fund to help make possible the sabbatical released time. Dean Jim L. Waits of the Candler School of Theology at Emory has most graciously seen to it that my writing efforts received full institutional support in more than simply monetary ways. I also received a substantial grant from the Association of Theological Schools in the U.S. and Canada during the academic year 1984–85, a grant made possible through a program sponsored by the Association under the title "Issues in Theological Education." A grant from the Center of Theological Inquiry, Princeton, New Jersey, made possible resident study at the Center during the winter term, 1985. For all this institutional support of my research I am profoundly grateful.

A number of my colleagues at Emory have been most helpful in giving critical reactions and suggestions at a number of points in the course of the writing. I wish especially to thank Rodney J. Hunter, Richard Osmer, William Mallard, and James W. Fowler for their careful reading of various drafts of chapters of the manuscript. I am particularly indebted to Bill Mallard for sparking and encouraging my interest over several years in the possibilities for recovery of theological undergirding for pastoral care to be found in narrative theology. The particular development of those and other ideas found in these pages I must take responsibility for myself, but the honing of those ideas could not have taken place without my Emory colleagues' help and critical support.

Finally, I wish to acknowledge the continuing stimulation I received from my students as I have attempted to formulate this approach to pastoral theology. Without the lively interaction and searching inquiry of seminarians, doctoral students, and parish pastors, my own search for widened horizons for pastoral work would have been both more lonely and less informed by the realistic dilemmas of ministry in the modern world.

Introduction
Widening Horizons by Redefining the Task: Pastoral Care and Practical Theology

Not so very many years ago, it might well have been argued that there was very little new under the sun insofar as pastoral care theory was concerned. The great resurgence of both interest in and newfound horizons for pastoral care ministry that had blossomed forth in the 1940s and 1950s—interests and horizons that enticed persons like myself into the field because they seemed to offer exciting new possibilities for making ministry more relevant to human needs—had seemingly run its course. All the necessary books about the basic meaning of caring pastorally and about such common pastoral care concerns as death and grief ministry, marital and premarital counseling, counseling alcoholics and their families, and the like seemed to have been written and rewritten. Even though the Rogerian methodology that had so dominated the expansion period of the 1950s and early 1960s had been largely superseded by a veritable toolbox of new methodologies coming from the psychotherapeutic world, the likelihood of anything truly new on the horizon by way of basic pastoral *care* theory seemed remote at best. Pastoral care as a discipline, while clearly established as one of the disciplines of ministry in virtually all theological schools, no longer enjoyed a position on the cutting edge of ministry.

Many factors went into that shift in the position of pastoral care among the disciplines of ministry, not least of which was the surge of concern for the great societal issues of racism and nuclear holocaust. Many persons outside the field began to think that pastoral care, while perhaps important for the day-to-day work of the parish pastor, was not equipped to encounter prophetically the larger public issues of the day. There also developed a disquieting awareness that pastoral care in its modern period had been in significant ways captive to the psychological-mindedness that had helped bring upon American culture the age of preoccupation with the self.

These and other factors in the movement of social and cultural history have indeed drastically altered the situation in which pastoral care as a discipline of ministry now finds itself. The discipline, like the society in which it developed in the modern period, is in a state of transition and flux. One of the encouraging signs of the times, however, is that pastoral care theorists increasingly are searching for theological roots, probing for the primary sources of the discipline's identity. This book is best seen as one such effort to relocate pastoral care practice within the tradition from which it sprang.

I must quickly add that it is not my purpose to engage in polemics. I have no desire to denigrate or discard the fruits of pastoral care's modern period. Rather, my search is for a fresh vision of what the discipline of pastoral care involves, while at the same time preserving the gains of the past forty years, including the appropriation of psychological ways of thinking about human needs and problems. Those gains must and can continue to be valued and capitalized upon, even while they are relativized by the recognition that the historical process has brought changes at many levels that affect the shape of pastoral care for the immediate future.

This bias from which I write has behind it a particular understanding of human history. It is a bias that links closely human individual and corporate identity with the narratives that have historically shaped those identities, giving them purpose and direction.[1] Yet those storied identities are constantly bombarded by the changes of the historical process. Because the human historical process never stands still, human needs constantly change. Not only that, but our ways of thinking about human needs are constantly in flux. So the narratives that have shaped our historical identity are continually experienced in a greater or lesser degree of tension with changing needs and emerging ways of thinking about those needs. So, too, pastors and pastoral care theorists must constantly have one ear open to the shifts that take place in the ways persons experience their needs and problems of living and the other open to the currents of change in ways of understanding and interpreting human needs.[2] Both these listenings need always to be kept in an intentional and sometimes intense dialogue with what the Christian tradition has historically said about human needs and problems and their relationship to issues of faith. Just why that is the case will, I hope, be made clear in the pages that follow.

In his cogent analysis of the perceptions that shaped the pastoral care and counseling movement in the period following World War II, historian E. Brooks Holifield says that two awarenesses were determinative. The first, an interpretive awareness that had been taking shape all through the twentieth century, had to do with the priority placed on self-realization. The metaphors that best caught up the primary human strivings all tended to emphasize one or another aspect of that historically shaped human purpose. Self-actualization, self-fulfillment, self-determination, self-motivation—no matter what the words might be, they all pointed to the realization of the self and the self's potentials. The second awareness was that many if not most corporate institutions and structures of society were experienced as interfering with rather than supporting the fulfillment of the self.[3]

In the cultural atmosphere shaped by the conflict between self-realization and burgeoning corporate structures perceived as interfering with that realization, pastoral response to the needs of persons became also, says Holifield, primarily concerned with responding to individual self-actualization issues. Pastors, many of them inheritors of American modes of Protestant piety, adopted the psychological idiom of the time. Helping persons to free themselves from family constraints, the moralistic constraints of social class respectability, and whatever interference with the realization of individual freedom might be coming from corporate authorities of one kind or another became a central function of pastoral care.

This organizing interpretation of pastoral care as response to human need for self-realization shaped to a considerable degree even those traditional aspects of pastoral care having to do with the care of the sick and the dying, the bereaved, and those in situational or relational crisis. These experiences of pain, suffering, and conflict were most often interpreted in psychological self-fulfillment terms. Death came to be seen as that ultimate existential block to self-realization; bereavement was given meaning as a time of incorporation of a loss of relationship into self-understanding in order that, the work of grief completed, the person might move on to further experiences of self-development and new relationships. Other common human crises were likewise cast into the molds provided by the languages of the self.[4]

Again, this is not to say that all efforts of the past few decades to adapt pastoral care to an age of self-realization were necessarily wrong or misguided. Certainly much good has come from using psychological ways of thinking about human needs. Because of the careful and sensitive work of pastors informed by psychology, countless persons have achieved liberation from moralistic conscience, inappropriate dependence upon parental authorities, the demands of oppressive expectations of others, and the like. These gains need to be preserved. Wherever and whenever pastors encounter persons who are suffering from the ills that block self-realization, they will continue to profit from viewing those problems within a psychological frame of reference. However, the difficulties spawned by an age of the self now need to be addressed.

Before we move to consider these difficulties, it seems important to share one reflection on pastoral care's involvement in the self-realization ethic. It would seem, looking back, that if there were shortcomings in the appropriation of self-realization psychologies for pastoral care, they were largely at the point of failure sufficiently to keep the newfound psychological perspectives in tension with the primary metaphors that have shaped the Christian tradition. I speak here of both the primary metaphors concerning human personhood and those that shaped the meaning of pastoral care in the tradition. I shall have more to say about both those matters.

The pastoral care field now is confronted by a radically changed situation from that which confronted the pastoral pioneers of what is generally thought of as the modern of psychologically enlightened period. Our new historical time is marked by several more or less radically new social realities that greatly complicate the practice of pastoral care. Many of these changes in our social situation have already been written and spoken about, not only by pastors and other theologians but by secular observers of the social scene.[5] The recognition of a changed social time has even permeated the popular media and is, some would say, indicated in such things as the outcome of recent elections and debates about such public issues as welfare budgets and tax policies!

These evidences of an important shift in the social context within which pastoral care practitioners must now work may be seen as having a number of significant elements, all of which are interrelated. Taken together, they make up a more or less radical alteration in the contextual matrix and a more or less radical change in the manner in which human pain evoking care is experienced. A list of those elements follows. Each of them will figure significantly in later proposals concerning the most appropriate mode of pastoral response for our time.

1. The *pluralism* that has come upon Western culture involves a pluralism of values and, perhaps even more significantly, a pluralism of languages for interpretation of what human life in the world is about. This means that Christian language for interpreting the meaning of things, evaluating human actions and attitudes, and formulating human purposes is now only one language among many and no longer can claim consensual legitimation. Furthermore, pluralism has now so penetrated every nook and cranny of Western social life that given individuals in the course of their normal activities on a given day may be required to move from one social context governed by one primary language of interpretation to another governed by another, and, often, to yet a third or fourth. This makes not only for fragmentation of language worlds among members of a social context but also for fragmentation within the day-to-day experience of the individual.

My favorite example of a person caught in the fragmentation brought about by pluralism involves a young man who came for pastoral counseling because he felt confused about who he wanted to be. He had been brought up in a conservative southern home in a small community where the family went to church regularly, both on Sunday and during the week. He attended the "training union" of his local church faithfully through high school and then went off to the state university, where he joined a college fraternity and was introduced to a very different way of life. After college he was employed in a large bank in his state's largest city and soon learned both to dress conservatively and to attend carefully to the bottom-line profit expectations of his employer. As he received sufficient promotions to afford it, he moved into a large apartment complex designed for the avant-garde single life-style. There he met and married an Irish Catholic girl from Boston who had come south to escape the close confines of her family. Before and after marriage, the young man continued to visit his parents biweekly, still attending church with them, now over his bride's objections. What seems at first glance almost a caricature of pluralism is, upon reflection, probably not unusual in the modern world. Whimsical scenarios of possible conflicts that might occur in this young man's daily life quickly produce intimations of the confusing variety of interpretive languages, not only about what is right and valuable but also about what "the real world" is that he confronts daily.

2. Clearly the young man into whose pluralistic life we have

quickly dipped shows what Don Browning has called the *loss of moral context*. There is certainly apt to be little consensus on moral values among his parents, his hard-nosed businessman boss, his fellow dwellers in the singles complex, and the deeper recesses of his wife's Irish Catholic upbringing. His confusion is, though he would perhaps have difficulty saying so, fundamentally moral. Not only that, but the various worlds he moves among in the course of daily life each comprise a moral universe whose values are taken for granted and unquestioned. To which of these worlds is he finally to belong? Or, what is more likely, is he simply to live chameleonlike in fragments of worlds, not fully identified with any?

3. Our young man of the several worlds also is suggestive of a popularly followed "solution" to the problem of fragmentation spoken of by some social scientists as *tribalism*.[6] People with the interpretive mind-set of the young man's parents will tend to stay within the same social and meaning-affirming group and will use various devices to insulate themselves from differing perspectives on the world. So, too, will persons immersed in the corporate business world or the youth culture. Thus to the confusion of having to move through several interpretive and value worlds in a single day is added the confusion of divided tribal loyalties. In this situation the boundaries of meaning worlds tend to break down, and consequently efforts to maintain them are undertaken with a rigidity that speaks of anxiety or even panic.

4. *Privatism* is another "solution" to fragmentation in the midst of pluralism, less prone to the insulation of tribal loyalty because it is more accommodating to the social realities. Life and meaning worlds are divided as neatly as possible into the public and the private. The public life of business and work, social club, and political involvement may require one set of value loyalties. Meanwhile, in the so-called private realm, very different and often contradictory values and perceptions may be at work. One might think of this as a controlled or limited fragmentation, resulting in frequent value and meaning conflicts which are more or less taken as inevitable, demanding tolerance and flexibility. Modern identity then becomes, as sociologist Peter Berger suggests, "peculiarly differentiated."[7]

5. Further and perhaps more ominous evidence of the impact of rapid change and pluralism on Western culture has been accumulating for some years now in the *altered patterns of psychopathology*. It has long been observed by psychotherapeutic professionals that the kinds of psychopathology evidenced in

those who seek professional help provide a barometer of the conflicts and deep issues of the society. Freud's hysterical patients embodied in extreme form the conflicts over sexuality of Victorian Europe at the turn of the century. The high incidence of obsessive-compulsive disorders in America during the mid-twentieth century reflected in subtle ways the Protestant work ethic piety of that society.

In recent years the primary concern of the psychotherapeutic community has turned toward persons who are variously described as borderline, persons suffering from problems of narcissism and faulty character formation lacking a firm sense of self. Though there are subtle differences among theorists concerning the nature and etiology of these disorders, there is general consensus that persons suffering from them have great difficulty sustaining a firm sense of selfhood, meaningful relationships with others, and an adequate working grasp of reality. In short, they are persons flawed and fragmented at deep levels in their personhood. The psychoanalyst who has perhaps most cogently related the high incidence of this form of psychopathology to the social conditions of contemporary Western culture is Heinz Kohut. In his book *The Restoration of the Self*, Kohut labels persons who have not yet been influenced profoundly by the changed social situation "Guilty Man," "Self-expressive Man," or "Creative Man." By these terms Kohut means that these persons suffer from the conflicts developed in a social situation that is still coherently sure of itself with regard to good and evil. They are relatively able to be self-expressive and creative, though they suffer from conflicts with social or familial norms. More recently, however, Kohut says that psychotherapeutic professionals have been confronted with what he terms "Tragic Man"—persons who are tragically flawed at the most primary levels in the formation of the nuclear self.[8]

Even though pastors will not ordinarily expect to be working at the intense and intimate level at which psychotherapeutic professionals work with individuals such as Heinz Kohut describes, they can expect to encounter many people in the course of their daily work whose problems of living stem from this level of disordered selfhood. In subtle ways, problems of this nature that are not severe enough to precipitate a search for psychotherapeutic assistance will be evident in unhappy interpersonal relationships, questions about personal faith, and empty feelings of purposelessness. To the extent that persons are experiencing these flaws in self-development, their perceptions and experience of the world will be skewed and their interpretations of reality and meaning marred by self-negation, swings from positive to strongly negative outlook, distorted self-reference, and the like.

While the social context has been changing as I have outlined, the pastoral care and counseling movement has been developing a roughly parallel awareness of identity concerns. During the last two decades the pastoral care field has been, at least to a degree, threatened with fragmentation. At one level we have seen pastoral counseling specialists, many now referring to themselves as "pastoral psychotherapists," separating themselves from parish pastors and becoming preoccupied with the development of a tribal guild in competition with other therapeutic guilds. (It should be noted that, recognizing the isolation that resulted from this heavy emphasis on psychotherapeutic specialization, the guild has now moved to admit parish pastors with appropriate qualifications in pastoral counseling to its ranks.) At another level, the pastoral care and counseling practitioner, whether parish pastor or counseling specialist, has been bombarded with a variety that often threatened to become a confusion of methodologies, most of them borrowed from secular theories and therapies. Conflict between those declaring "family systems theory" as the methodological standard of choice and those following a Rogerian or psychoanalytically oriented methodology, to name but one or two sets of divisions, has resulted in some confusion concerning not only what pastoral counseling is but what the pastor is most appropriately called to do with persons who come seeking help.

Happily, as recognition of the identity problems within pastoral care and counseling has increased, there has come a strong call for recovery of pastoral care and counseling's theological rootage. This move toward reconsideration of rootage is a significant one in more than simply the obvious sense that theology is central to all forms of ministry. Hermeneutically speaking, it signals an awareness that identity is linked to origins, most particularly origins that supply the deep metaphors and meanings that tell us who we are. A recovery of identity, be it by an individual or a corporate group such as pastoral care practitioners, always involves a return to the deep narrative structures that have carried from generation to generation the meanings involved in belonging to a particular people.

My earlier book, *The Living Human Document: Re-visioning Pastoral Counseling in a Hermeneutical Mode*, developed a prolegomenon to a theory of pastoral counseling that makes use of some of the tools and concepts now available from the field of interpretation theory, most particularly philosophical hermeneutics. That theory seeks to recover pastoral counseling's Christian theological roots while yet maintaining the dialogue with the psychological and social sciences from which pastoral care and counseling have gained so much during recent decades. Drawing upon psychoanalytic object relations theory (Kohut and others), I developed the notion that the self, in the particularity of its experiences of living from birth, develops a narrative or "story of the self" that, at the deepest levels, is connected to the larger narratives and their metaphors of the context into which the individual has been born. This psychological and hermeneutical way of thinking about the self has important linkages with the concept of pilgrimage as it has been considered in the Judeo-Christian tradition. Theologically, individual and corporate human pilgrimages are linked to the narrative structure of that tradition's story of the relationship of God to the world.

The present book attempts to extend and further clarify the hermeneutical perspective on pastoral care and counseling in several important ways. First and most obviously, I am shifting the immediate context to be considered from the formally structured *counseling* relationship between the pastoral counselor and one or a few persons to the more informal and differently structured context of pastoral *care* in the parish and its surrounding community. Second, I will explore further the significance and implications of human life's narrative structure, joining with those in cultural anthropology, literary criticism, and what has come to be called narrative theology in affirming that humans structure meaning and hold in coherence the diverse elements of experience by means of a narrative structure. For Christians that means taking with great seriousness the historic biblical narratives that have shaped the tradition of the people of God.

But the pluralistic context of modern life presses persons and communities to live out multiple stories, often in ways that cut across each other. Here we encounter the common need for a grounding or primary narrative out of which come models for interpreting life situations, making choices among conflicting values, and maintaining a core of identity while fulfilling multiple roles shaped by differing rules and models of what is good and useful.

If pastoral care must at all times be sensitive to the particularity of human needs, then the situation of radical pluralism in which we now find ourselves has great significance for what pastors should be keeping at the center of their attention. To take the pluralistic situation seriously, pastors will need to widen the

horizon of their pastoral interests from the concern with psychological and relational well-being that has been the focus of the
recent past. This does not mean negating or neglecting the
importance of pastoral care as related to crisis ministry. But it
does mean that the pain of human need to which pastoral care
must respond should include and perhaps even emphasize the
pain and confusion produced by living at this particular time in
our culture. It means widening the horizon of pastoral concern
to include the often unspoken and even unrecognized concerns
of ordinary folk as they go about the business of their lives in a
social situation that has become fragmented and no longer supports them in their efforts to live as the people of God. It is to this
deep and pervasive social malaise that pastoral care must now
respond.

Among theologians who have considered this problem of modern life, perhaps none has been more helpful in offering clarifying guidance than H. Richard Niebuhr. In his book *The Responsible
Self*, he grapples with the problem of the meaning of responsibility in an increasingly pluralistic world in which legalisms and
narrowly constructed frameworks for human choice and action
no longer function. His use of the metaphor of responsibility
provides him a way of both comprehending the complexity of
that social situation and finding a way to consistent moral
action.[9] For Niebuhr the first element of responsibility is simply
the idea of response. Responsible action, whatever the situation
might be, is action in response to action upon us. The situation
we are in acts upon us, creates the necessity of response. But,
says Niebuhr, our response always involves our interpretation of
the meaning of the situation that acts upon us. Human response
is always interpreted response or response to an interpretation
of "what is going on." Whatever is going on must first be put into
some framework of meaning. Here, of course, is the crux of the
problem of pluralism. What language for talking about what is
going on in a given situation is to provide an organizing or
overarching framework of meaning? For Niebuhr this question
has to do with accountability and social solidarity. To be responsible is to respond in a framework of accountability to those
whose actions call forth my response and with whom I am in
solidarity, because we together make up a continuing society.[10]

We will return later to the thought of H. Richard Niebuhr. Here
it is important to say that for Niebuhr the society with which we
are finally in solidarity is that society accountable to God. "I
place my companions, human and subhuman and superhuman,
in the one universal society which has its center neither in me

nor in any finite cause but in the Transcendent One." Or, again: "Responsibility affirms: 'God is acting in all actions upon you. So respond to all actions upon you as to respond to his action.' "[11]

If one listens closely to these signs for the road ahead coming from theologians such as H. Richard Niebuhr, one hears at work a hermeneutical frame of reference and response rooted in the narrative structure at the core of the Judeo-Christian tradition. It is the story of the transcendent God who creates, promises to be faithful, and calls God's people into covenant relationship with one another and with their Creator. From that story are drawn the primary metaphors that tell us who we are and what our responses to our situation should be. What follows on these pages is an attempt to explore in some depth what being responsible and faithful to that story means for pastoral care in a pluralistic, often fragmented, but fermenting and potentially creative time.

The word *pastoral* itself contains two major connotations that give shape to what pastoral care is about. On the one hand, the word *pastoral* connotes a particular source or origin for the care that is being given. That source is found in a particular community of which the pastoral person is a representative. The person does not come to the situation of care with simply a general intention of goodwill but, rather, with the meanings and desires of the community he or she represents. On the other hand, the word *pastoral* connotes response to particular persons in particular situations. Again, this particularity means that the one who gives care is not simply attempting to respond to something so broad and general as "the needs of humankind." No, there is a particularity about the persons and the situations toward which the pastoral care is directed.

This suggests that pastoral care is given its particularity by the historical process in which it is embedded. The actions that are understood as pastoral will differ from one time in history to another depending upon the particular historical consciousness of the time and place in which it occurs. That historical particularity has to do with both connotations of the word *pastoral,* what it means to represent the community of faith and what it means to respond to the particularity of human need. To say it even more simply and generally, we begin with the notion that pastoral care changes the particularity of its focus in relation to the changes of the historical process.

That notion about historical change in pastoral care needs to be balanced with another understanding with which it is always in a degree of tension. For pastoral care to remain pastoral, there must be a certain deep continuity of meaning at its core. One cannot simply do whatever one desires or whatever seems appropriate in a particular situation, whatever that might be, and call that action pastoral. A connection must be maintained with the deepest meanings of what that word denotes. Those deepest meanings are most often metaphorical and come from the narratives, the stories, that are remembered as having produced the metaphors. While much more will be said about metaphor and narrative later, it will suffice here to say that the tension between deep historical meanings of pastoral care and the particular meaning of pastoral care actions in a given historical situation remains a problem that always must be given attention.

This book will address the problem by constructing an undergirding practical theology for pastoral care that gives particular attention to the importance of the narrative structure of human experience. Because pastoral care practice is always in some way representative ministry, it must give particular attention to the meaning of pastoral acts as they can be understood by using the languages and meanings that flow from the Christian community and its tradition. Pastoral care is therefore always under the obligation to be grounded in theology. But pastoral theology is fundamentally practical. It finds its task and purpose in the practical reality of situations that call for pastoral response. It is always a theology that emerges from reflection on a practical situation.

The practical theology to be constructed is, methodologically speaking, best termed a narrative hermeneutical practical theology. Technical as that phrase may sound, it simply means that the approach to practical theology here taken assumes two things as being of primary importance: (1) Meanings attached to situations involving humans and human actions in situations are always grounded in some narrative structure. They emerge from some story or cluster of stories as to why things happen and what they mean. (2) Questions concerning how those situations and humans in those situations are being interpreted are therefore of primary importance in understanding and responding to any situation involving humans. Interpretation connects the particularity of presenting situations with the long story that tells how situations are to be understood. Interpretation not only precedes human action; human actions are themselves expressions of interpretations.

Chapter 1 introduces practical pastoral theology and initiates reflection on the present situation confronting pastoral care practitioners: the situation of many persons influenced in peculiar ways by the pluralism and fragmentation of modern life. That situation is opened up primarily by means of two broad case studies. Some preliminary soundings of the potential value of the narrative hermeneutical approach to practical theology are tested. A primary goal for pastoral care is set forth as the pastoral facilitation of Christian life in the modern world. Chapter 2 delves more deeply into some of the important dimensions of contemporary approaches to theology built upon the notion that theologies explicate and objectify stories of God and the world. Chapter 3 proposes a narrative hermeneutical structure for practical theology in some detail, as well as in several schematizations. That structure is then tested in chapter 4 by detailed examination of a typical case example of a pastoral ministry problem. Chapter 5 undertakes a phenomenological study of the task of pastoral care conceived within the practical theological structure that has been developed. A brief Epilogue concludes the book with an agenda of issues and tasks that emerge as implications of the now-widened horizons for pastoral care.

I have taken the reader on this walk-through of the book in order to provide a kind of map of the territory to be explored. If I may continue for a moment the metaphor of a walk, the terrain before us to be explored is not easy to enter or cross. Our walk will not be an effortless stroll on a beaten path. It will rather be more like a hike in mountainous country that has been previously explored by other hikers with differing purposes from ours, but which has not yet been well mapped and prepared. Some vistas will have a familiar appearance; others will seem strange and perhaps even uninviting. As guide on the hike, I propose to highlight landmarks and points of interest along the way as well as to make the appropriate connections with what is already known to be good pastoral care practice. Not all issues—side trips—will be mapped and cleared. But the main path toward the goal of formulating a genuinely Christian narrative practical theology for pastoral care will, I trust, be traversed.

Let us begin by looking carefully at the situation in American culture that confronts us, the situation that shapes the problem of praxis for pastoral care in our time.

1
Story and Goal:
Christian Life in the Modern World

The Introduction makes the simple assertion that the word *pastoral* itself contains the tensions of meaning that shape the task of pastoral care. On the one hand, the word speaks of a community of persons whose identity as a community is shaped by a certain way of seeing the world. The pastor is one who represents that community and its meanings. On the other hand, the word *pastoral* contains the intention of the community to respond to the particularity of the needs of persons within its care. The pastor's work takes place in the movement back and forth in the tension between those two sides of meaning.

The word *pastoral* contains, however, not only a representational meaning shaped by a community with a shared tradition and an intention concerning particularly of human need, but also a goal, an eschatological purpose, if you will. It looks toward a future, a future envisioned by the community's story, which the community seeks to share with all persons. Thus the pastoral task lies not only in the tension between the community's way of seeing the world and the particularity of present human need, but also in the tension between particular present human needs and the possibilities of fulfillment of human needs that the community's story envisions.

In this chapter I want to break open what must seem to be a rather cryptic, loaded definition of the meaning of the word *pastoral* in several ways that will be important later. First, I want to speak briefly about the theory of narrative which underlies my definition. That understanding of narrative and its importance for interpreting anything human plays a significant if not determinative role in what I want to say about a hermeneutical perspective on pastoral care. Second, building upon what can be said about the place of narrative generally in human experience, I want to turn our attention toward the theological significance for pastoral care of the particular narrative structure that shapes the Christian tradition and the community that carries that tradition within itself. The underlying purpose of these reflections is, as the title of the chapter suggests, to arrive at a vision of the goal of pastoral care in our present context, the modern world.

The Role of the Narrative Structure

To say that the word *pastoral* has behind or beneath it a narrative structure is to emphasize that the very word has gathered around it an aura of meaning that is nested in a story, a long story of a people. Without that story, the word *pastoral* would not have the meanings it has. The Bible is a collection of writings, many of them stories, that tells of the origins of that people. Thus all it means to be a member of the Christian community is rooted in the story of that community's origins and history.

What I have just said about the narrative structure of what it means to be a member of the Christian community is based upon an understanding of human experience that comes from a theory about all human communities—indeed, all human projects and activities. The theory is that all things human are in some sense rooted in, or find their deepest structural framework in, a narrative or story of some kind. This is true whether we are members of a self-consciously identified community such as the Christian community or are acting within some orientation to the world that is more or less taken for granted and not articulated as a story. Even the most scientific of modern people, those who may scoff at such "myths," as they may call them, as the notion that God created the universe, are themselves living and experiencing the world within a narrative structure. In their case it may be the story of the so-called big bang beginning of the cosmos and the evolution of planets and of living things. But, because even in science we deal not just with "facts" but with possibilities and hypotheses, a story of the way things are, have been, and will be is necessarily formed.

Stephen Crites has suggested that this narrative structure of all things human comes about because of the way we experience things in our everyday lives. Writing about this, he says:

> It is not that "reality" in itself somehow has a narrative form, but our experience does have. . . . For that matter, it is only when we don the cloak or the scientist's white coat (or some such garment reserved for deep thinking) that we make clear distinctions between

"reality" and what appears in "experience." Our common
Lebenswelt contains what we encounter in immediate experience
and deal with in our practical activity, to which narrative locution
is our most direct linguistic access. When we speak to or of what is
immediately real to us we tell stories and fragments of stories.
"Ordinary language" is largely made up of the sorts of locutions we
employ in telling stories. What we ordinarily recognize as real and
attempt practically to cope with is what we can put in narrative
language.[1]

The difference that Stephen Crites points to between the language we use in ordinary speech and that of the philosophers
and scientists is an important one. It reminds me to make clear
that when I say that all human activities have undergirding them
a narrative structure, I am not seeking to reduce everything
human to the language of story. The word *pastoral*, for example,
can be spoken about in other ways than the way of images linked
to the story of the use of that word in a community. Insofar as its
meaning is linked to the story of the Judeo-Christian community,
however, it is used metaphorically. That is to say, the experience
of the community shaped by that community's story has given
the word a certain cast of meaning. The word itself is a vessel
into which the storied history of the community has poured
certain meanings. But *pastoral* also can be analyzed in the manner of, for example, an analogy. In fact, in its beginnings in the
Judeo-Christian community, the word probably developed out of
an analogy—the analogy between the care of the shepherd for
the flock of sheep or goats and the care of the leader of a
community for the community's members. In fact, the usage
probably had its beginnings in a kind of double analogy, that of
the care of Yahweh for his people and the care of the shepherd
for the flock *and* that of the care of Yahweh for his people and
the care of the community for one another and for the world.

Historians of the development of language and narrative assign
considerable importance to the separation that occurred in the
course of history between the language of narrative and metaphor, on the one hand, and the language of science and philosophy, on the other. It is beyond the scope of our interest here to
detail that history, but the fact of the separation and its implications for modern life are important to acknowledge. At a very
practical level, pastors themselves are often caught between the
need to be carefully scientific and analytically factual about the
way they go about their work and the desire to be imaginative
and artful in pastoral relationships. The historians to whom I
refer would see this conflict as but one example of a pervasive

tension between factual, empirical, analytical modes of thought
and the more imaginative, softly focused mode of art and
storytelling.

Brian Wicker, in his book *The Story-shaped World*, speaks of
the division between these two ways of thinking and speaking in
this way:

> I want to maintain that neither is fully intelligible without reference
> to the other: for the relation of fact to fiction, of the real world to
> the world of story, is itself a kind of "metaphysical pact," a secret to
> which the narrator's art is the metaphorical key. . . . Pascal's famous
> opposition between the God of the Philosophers and the God of
> Abraham, Isaac, and Jacob is in the first place an opposition between
> styles of language. But Pascal knew well enough, as we do also, that
> the choice of a style is also the choice of a whole world-view. When
> the poets and story-tellers talked of God in the language of Mailer's
> "savages" [the reference here is to an earlier quotation from Norman
> Mailer], by way of metaphor, they were also choosing its accompa-
> nying metaphysic. Whereas, when the philosophers . . . spoke of
> Him they did so (if at all) in the sophisticated abstract language of
> geometrically defined objects and value-free physical laws.[2]

Wicker goes on to say that beginning with the medieval philosophical synthesis of Thomas Aquinas and others, the analytical,
philosophical language based fundamentally on a theory of analogy began to become dominant in the thinking and language of
the West at the expense of underplaying the importance of poetry
and storytelling, "that is to say, by undervaluing or even misun-
derstanding the role of *metaphorical* language."[3] Both kinds of
thought and language are needed, and they must be held in a
kind of tension which the philosopher-theologian Paul Ricoeur
has usefully spoken of as the tension between the language of
force and of meaning.[4]

Parish pastors may resonate with Wicker's concern for maintaining a balance between imaginative, poetic, metaphorical
thinking and philosophical and scientific forms of thought if the
difficulties posed by that concern can be seen as analogous to the
difficulties pastors often experience in the preparation of sermons. In sermon preparation, a tenuous balance must be maintained between clarity of the theological or ethical concepts that
undergird the sermon and the use of story, image, and metaphor
to so express the argument that it can be heard and appropriated
by the congregation. Sermons that lack story, image, and metaphor soon become abstract and disconnected from the living
stuff of life. But sermons that lack clear, logical undergirding
premises and careful analysis of human and theological prob-

lems soon become shallow and lack a firm objective grasp of the complex nature of theological truth. Each form of language reveals aspects of the problem being addressed not made apparent by the other. Each way of thinking and speaking is therefore necessary.

What is true concerning sermon preparation is likewise true of the work of pastoral care. Both careful and objective analysis and imaginative, intuitive framing of the problem in some essentially metaphorical construction are skills the good pastor must cultivate. Each is essential for good pastoral care. The pastor needs to be both poetic story sharer and theological, ethical, and/or scientific analyst.

As the argument of this book develops it will, I hope, become clear that one of my goals is to participate in the recovery of poetic, storylike language for pastoral care. It is not my wish to reduce everything about pastoral care to the language of story, but rather to explore with the reader some of the possibilities for envisioning pastoral care in our time by means of the appropriation of a language of metaphor and story. It should also be kept in mind, however, that an interest in recovering the language of metaphor and story in pastoral care has at its center a concern to take seriously the common language of the people for whom we care. "For we dream in narrative, daydream in narrative, remember, anticipate, hope, despair, believe, doubt, plan, revise, criticise, construct, gossip, learn, hate and love by narrative. In order to live, we make up stories about ourselves and others, about the personal as well as the social past and future."[5]

One further thing needs to be said about narrative generally before we move on to consider the particular narratives out of which the Judeo-Christian community has been formed. It is through narrative that we humans are able to transcend time. In fact, our experience of time has inherent in it a narrative structure.[6] The very notions of a past, a present, and a future are enfolded within a way of seeing time as a story with a beginning, a middle, and an end. We look back and look forward by means of an experience of time as story. Our present experience in time is given meaning as it is connected with what has gone on before in the story of our lives and the lives of humankind and what we anticipate may go on in the future. We quite literally live our lives in time because we are able to structure the passage of time as a story. It is thus primarily by our stories concerning human life in time that we are able to have a sense of the whole of things spanning past, present, and future.[7]

The Role of the Christian Narrative

The recognition that we humanize time and maintain a sense of the whole of things by means of story necessitates that we who identify ourselves as Christians reflect on the central narratives that have shaped Christian experience. Primarily, these are the stories of the Bible as, taken together, they make up the multi-faceted and pluralistic yet somehow unified narrative account of the relationship between God and the world. It is through these stories, together with their metaphorical images and themes, that we have constructed our primary understanding of who we are and who we were meant to be. Indeed, Northrop Frye, the distinguished literary critic who has perhaps done more than any other scholar in that field to attend to the history of narrative, declares that, not just for the Judeo-Christian community but for all of Western civilization, it is the deep narrative structures of the biblical witness that provide the lowest level of meaning from which all other narratives of the world either are drawn or take departure.[8]

It is just at this point that today's changed contextual situation affects the problem of pastoral care. As I indicated in the Introduction, following Don S. Browning and others, rapid social change and pluralism have so undermined this Judeo-Christian way of structuring the narrative and moral context that there is danger of the culture's losing track of the narrative meanings that Northrop Frye says have shaped it. Fragmentation has resulted in the significant loss of the connection between present lived experience and the grounding narratives that historically have given that experience meaning.[9] In that changed situation, an overriding task of pastoral care is assisting persons to sustain that context of meaning in all aspects of their lives, individually and corporately. Said another way, a primary goal of pastoral care, as well as its overriding problem, becomes that of finding ways to help persons to live in the modern world with a sustaining consciousness of the Judeo-Christian narrative that tells them who they are and who they are to be. The sustaining of that consciousness, however, must be done while still critically appropriating the best of knowledge and perspectives made possible by modern life.

While reflecting on this contextually defined problem of pastoral care in our time, I recall two different experiences. The first came to me, as it did to many other white persons, particularly in the American South, by way of a growing awareness through the time of racial desegregation of how the deeply rooted black

Christian identity had sustained black persons through years of oppression when they were continually given debasing and identity-destroying messages. Regardless of how the dominant white society may have identified them and hammered at their self-respect, many of them, though not all, were able to sustain a dignity and clarity about who they were. Through the powerful and articulate leadership of, most particularly, Martin Luther King, Jr., this was possible because even the oppression they experienced was enfolded in their minds within a meaning structure shaped by the Judeo-Christian narrative. "We shall overcome" was rooted in the story of the exodus of the people of God.

I worked for a number of years during the desegregation crisis in a metropolitan medical center serving a patient population made up of a high percentage of poor blacks. Again and again I heard unbelievably difficult life experiences given meaning and integrity by way of symbolic words and phrases drawn from the biblical story of the people of God. The worst kind of fragmentation in actual life experience was made both bearable and meaningful by the connection of that experience to these narrative symbols. Most often the connection was made naturally and without question. It was taken for granted.

The dignity and integrity of which I speak was, of course, not true of all the black people I encountered. Some seemed rather to have accepted the identity bestowed upon them by their social situation. Beaten down by the dehumanization of racism, they seemed either to have lost touch with or never to have established at a core level that identity as children of a faithful and loving God which sustained their fellow sufferers. Their identities had been shaped by other stories, other designations of their worth. Among these individuals, whose very appearance often spoke of their fragmented identity, I remember a beautiful young black girl, who asked me one day in a group conversation, "We have been told we are inferior; do you think that we really are?" It was an honest question asked seriously and earnestly. It contained no hostile challenge, only a desire for the truth. I could only answer her by reminding her of the God whom I tried to represent in my ministry. That God did not consider anyone "inferior." The picture of her lovely face and honest question will always be sharp and clear in my memory. I was confronted as I had not been before with the destructive power of white racism.

The second experience that I have come to see as an example of the problem of sustaining connections with the Judeo-Christian story comes from a book by an American historian, Philip Greven, titled *The Protestant Temperament*. Greven seeks to trace the connection between religious consciousness and patterns of family life and child care during the seventeenth, eighteenth, and nineteenth centuries of American life. Greven's argument is that throughout these centuries a pattern of three broad types of religious consciousness and accompanying modes of family life existed with considerable consistency. The types Greven delineates are the Evangelical, the Moderate, and the Genteel families.

Evangelical families, says Greven, were convinced of the fundamental depravity of human nature and of the necessity of an experience of the new birth. Accordingly, they structured family life around the central meanings of that narrative structure. The story of the family was made to conform to the story of fallen human nature. The parents, drawing their image of authority from the image of God of Authority and Judgment, ruled the family with justice and absolute power, demanding obedience and submission from the children. The purpose of family life for the young child was to prepare the way for the new birth by providing the child with the prerequisite, a broken spirit of contrition. Guilt, self-examination, great attention to inner motivation, and much concern for right behavior, accompanied by largely hidden resentment, rebellion, and self-assertion, were the result of family life shaped by this consciousness.

Moderate families, says Greven, emphasized parental "bending of the will" by love and example, rather than the harsher breaking of the spirit of the child. Conformity of life to the will of God and the patterns of a godly life were still the goal, but, because the appropriation of the biblical narrative images were skewed in the direction of the love of God, rather than God's authority and judgment, the dominant mode of parental relationship was softer and more subtly controlling. This pattern also had its accompanying developmental problems. Guilt was ever-present, as with the Evangelical children, but here accompanied by a peculiar fear of falling short of the mark of perfection set lovingly but firmly by the parents.

Greven's picture of the Genteel family is one of less preoccupation with either the image of the naturally depraved soul of the child or the bending of the child's spirit. Rather, the Genteel parents seemed to assume the basic goodness of the child's natural spirit and to encourage its full expression. Childhood was a time for self-expression and exploration, often in rambunctious and undisciplined ways. In fact, life was a gift of God to be enjoyed and developed to the fullest. Grace, rather than law and obedience, was what was taken for granted. Beneath this consciousness and its mode of family life could be found a very different story of the relationship of human life to the life of God, a more exuberant, if at times irresponsible story. Genteel families were preoccupied not with the state of the soul but with the everyday affairs of an active and largely unreflective life.[10]

Some evidence of the continuation of patterns of family life structured historically out of differing interpretations of basic themes of the Judeo-Christian story can be found in social-scientific studies of family systems that have been made in recent years. Family systems theorists posit a largely hidden systemic structure that monitors and controls family interaction in firmly established patterns. One of the more useful of such studies, this one of so-called "normal" families, is that done by the social scientists David Kantor and William Lehr titled *Inside the Family*.[11] Like Philip Greven, Kantor and Lehr develop a typology of family system styles. Some families structure their life-style in the manner of a closed system. That is to say, all family behavior is closely and carefully regulated within a stable and set authority hierarchy, most often paternalistic though sometimes with the mother as the final arbiter of family rules. Management of time and activities is relatively rigid. Interaction between family members and the outside world is likewise carefully controlled.

Kantor and Lehr delineate a second type of family structure as the open family. Here the family interactions with one another and with the outside world are much more democratic and governed by individual choice, while the family still maintains a more or less close family loyalty. Decisions are made not so much by the exercise of parental authority as by the result of family discussion and group decision. Parents arbitrarily intervene only in situations of impasse or when basic family values are at stake. The system is open, freely spontaneous, and yet regulated and consistent.

The third type of family structure posited by these social scientists is, as might be expected, the random family. In contrast to closed and open families, here there is little organizational structure or consistent regulation of family interactions. Individuality and spontaneity are given full expression and encouraged. Irregular hours, irregular meals, irregular scheduling of activities is the norm. Each family member is expected to regulate his or her own life, with little attention to the priorities or needs of the family as a whole.

Kantor and Lehr, working out of their social-scientific perspective, make no value judgments as to which of these three types of families is the most viable or, ethically speaking, best as a model for family life in the modern world. Neither do they speculate as to the cultural origins of these patterns as they have uncovered them. From our perspective, however, one cannot help wondering if what these studies have uncovered is not the twentieth-century residual of the religiously grounded patterns of which Philip Greven has written.

As I have used Philip Greven's theory concerning the fundamental images that have shaped American family life in my teaching, particularly in comparison with studies of twentieth-century families made by social scientists like David Kantor and William Lehr, one question has consistently recurred to me and to my students: What has happened to the narrative structure of the images of family life that seem to be at work in many families we encounter today? Patterns resembling those identified by Greven seem still to be present. With some families, most notably those Greven would identify as Evangelical, the connection between religious consciousness and child-rearing pattern still remains fairly clear, though some children of these families have great difficulty making the transition from the authority of the family to the social situation of independent "autonomous" living legitimated by society. Even with some so-called Evangelical families, and most certainly with families exhibiting more Moderate or Genteel patterns of child-rearing (open and random, in Kantor and Lehr's categories), my students and I observe that the connection between child-rearing practice and religious consciousness has been to a great extent lost. Not only do the patterns of child rearing seem less and less consistent, but, even more pervasively, the religious rationale that supports and structures whatever pattern exists in parental behavior seems vague or nonexistent. For some, of course, whatever rationale there may be has been largely psychologized in the popular language of the time. At any rate, the connection between behavioral patterning of family life and historic religious consciousness seems to have largely disappeared.

Both observation of black experience and family child-rearing patterns would thus seem to bear out two things I have said earlier. In each case there seem to be deep-lying narrative images and themes that undergird interpretive and behavioral patterns. And in each case, there exists the omnipresent threat of the disappearance of the experienced connection between pattern and narrative source. The sustaining and, where necessary, restoration of those connections seem clearly to be high priorities for pastoral care seen as response to the particularity of human need at a given time. They become priorities dictated both by the representational task of pastoral care vis-à-vis the Judeo-Christian story and by the particular human needs evidenced in our time. An effort at restoration does not mean attempting to get families to go back to the patterns of family life of the seventeenth or eighteenth centuries. The twentieth-century context is a very different one. But the recovery of the biblical narrative sources of ways of attending to the issues of family interactions is crucial, if life in the family is to remain undergirded by Christian meanings.

Competing Narratives in American Life

Before moving on to consider, at least in a preliminary fashion, some of the central narrative biblical themes that should undergird Christian life in the modern world, I want first to sketch briefly some of the competing stories that are at work in shaping American cultural life. Some of these narrative themes are best understood as skewed distortions of older interpretive images that have their origins in the Judeo-Christian story. Some, however, are themes that are more clearly drawn from the scientific-technological and corporate business worlds and their underlying interpretations of the purposes of modern life.

If we examine closely the observations of family life by both the historian and the social scientists summarized in the preceding section, an interesting and potentially useful dialectical tension seems evident. On the one hand, there is the pull toward corporate and traditional control of behavior and attitude toward self and world. Evangelical and closed families seem clearly "conservative" in this regard. There are ways of living and being that they want deeply to preserve. A loyalty to a "way of life" provides a hermeneutical key to a way of seeing everything that goes on, both in the family and in the world at large. Interpretations of decisions, actions, values, attitudes, and the like are all colored by loyalty to this way of seeing. Moderate and open families likewise exhibit similar loyalties to a communally affirmed way of life. On the other hand, there is the pull toward individuality, freedom of self-determination, free involvement of the self in a world of self-determined relationships. Genteel and random families most clearly exhibit this high value placed on individuality. In sum, there is an evident tension between the primacy of the self and the primacy of a corporate community and its tradition.

Robert Bellah, writing in a volume of collected essays about the sects and cults that developed out of the upheaval of the 1960s in American life, says that two underlying interpretations of reality have been most prevalent and successful in providing meaning and generating loyalty in American life: biblical religion and utilitarian individualism.[12] According to Bellah, the American interpretation of biblical religion has been shaped largely out of a self-understanding of the original colonists that they were "God's new Israel," a chosen people who were to make a new beginning to fulfill the promise of God for God's covenant people. From this interpretation of the biblical narrative grew what Bellah terms American civil religion, a concept he elaborates more fully in his book *The Broken Covenant.*[13] From this American vision of covenant grew many of the images both of progressivism and of the special relationship of America with God and the world.

The other interpretation of reality which, Bellah says provided a center of interpretive loyalty in American life was that of "utilitarian individualism." This interpretive understanding was not fully compatible with the biblical covenant tradition and, according to Bellah, was rooted rather in sophistic, skeptical, and hedonist strands of ancient Greek philosophy, as modified by such persons as John Locke and Thomas Hobbes.[14]

Reflecting on the tension between self-direction and family loyalty as found in the work of Greven and of Kantor and Lehr, one cannot help wondering if the interplay of the two interpretive themes Bellah has identified has not played an important role in determining the conflicts that are pulling and tugging in the life of the American family. If this be the case, perhaps we can identify a central underlying problematic theme for pastoral care, not only of families and individuals in modern life but of other levels of corporate life as well.

Recognition of this tension—between the primacy and autonomy of the self ("individuation," in the words of many developmental psychologists) and of the corporate group and commonly shared values and interpretive meanings—has become commonplace in American popular culture in recent years. Whether that tension be labeled the contest between autonomy and heteronomy (by philosophers), between self-fulfillment and conformity (by psychologists), or between narcissism and group solidarity (by social psychologists), ordinary folk in American life today experience the bind of needing to be strong and self-sufficient and needing to belong. To live a Christian life in the modern world presents that problem in ways that are both common to the culture and peculiar to one who seeks to resolve the issue in Christian terms within a relationship to a community called Christian.

As Robert Bellah has suggested, this problem of modern life is involved to a considerable extent in the problem of pluralism described earlier. Interpretive images other than Judeo-Christian ones undergird the search for self-autonomy. Not only utilitarian individualism but more recent forms of individualism shaped by popular appropriation of psychology and the American dream of self-made success press moderns toward a self-fulfillment ethic as an organizing narrative structure for living. On the other hand, the corporate business world that now provides or withholds the means of attaining success for the individual has its own modes of demanding conformity and submission to a largely hierarchical corporate structure. The narratives that, at least on or near the surface, inform those structures seem clearly to have developed far beyond and remote from the Protestant work ethic connections with the biblical narrative structure about which Max Weber wrote.[15]

Having established, albeit somewhat sketchily, the importance of narrative structures for understanding the way we humans—in the West, at least—experience the flow of experience, and having underlined the central place of biblical narratives in the tradition of Western civilization generally as well as some of their permutations in American individual, family, and corporate life, I want now to turn to some preliminary reflections on those biblical narratives themselves.

The Biblical Narrative

To be Christian means for us to see ourselves, the world about us, and human purposes within the interpretive vision provided by the metaphors and themes of the Christian story. Our interpretations of that story will necessarily be different from our forebears', because we begin from our involvement in a very different time. Yet our interpretations will be in significant ways connected to theirs, not only because the deep metaphorical images of the Christian story are the same but also because in a peculiar way their story is our story. We are their descendants. The preliminary reflections here will be developed further in later chapters.

Theological reflection, wherever and whenever it occurs, always begins within an immediate social context. We begin with the questions and intimations that come to us out of our involvement in our own time and place. Theological reflection cannot begin, hard as we may try, from some ahistorical point of departure or even from some historical point remote from our own.

We can attempt to make a transcendent leap to another time and place, perhaps to the time of beginnings of the historical process in which we are located, but our beginning place is from the standpoint of our time, our place. That being the case, let us begin our preliminary theological reflection with the two examples I used to illustrate the presence and threatened dissolution of deep narrative themes.

From the story of black persons comes a compelling question: From where did these people get their confidence in their Christian identity? Asked another way, how did they know that the God of their faith would be with them come what may in their present situation of oppression and suffering? They seemed able to enfold whatever experience life brought to them within a storied structure that assumed God would not forsake them. Their identity was shaped by that confidence. Where did that confidence come from?

One of the oldest of biblical narrative themes comes immediately to mind, which shaped one aspect of the Old Testament covenant tradition. In capsule form it is simply, "I will be your God and you shall be my people." It is the story of God's promise of faithfulness in every circumstance. For black people suffering from subjugation to racism, it is perhaps most powerfully linked to the story of the children of Israel in slavery and God's delivering them from bondage. The oppressed are liberated from their oppressors. But beneath or within that image of deliverance is the image of God's faithful and suffering presence with God's people. Somewhere in the consciousness of the poor black persons I met in the hospital who had managed to retain their dignity and integrity, that narrative theme was at work, with both its pain and its hope, its lament and its stubborn insistence on retaining a sense of significance before God and other humans. Life, even impossibly difficult life, was given meaning and significance because it was lived within that story. The story of their life was nested in the story of the people of God. As more than one old and worn black woman said to me out of her situation of illness and worry about what was to happen to her family, "God's not gonna put more on you than you can bear! God's gonna make it come out right in the end." Such affirmations of faith were often accompanied by a lament: "How long, O Lord, how long!" That, too, told of a story of a God with whom one could contend, to whom one could legitimately direct demanding questions. No far-off, distant, and uncommunicative God this!

A whole cluster of theological questions hover in the background as one reflects on this appropriation of the biblical covenant narrative by the black persons of my memory. What is the meaning of God's faithfulness? Of God's "presence" with these people? On what basis are we to respond to their affirmation of the faithfulness of God in the face of the unspoken, impatient doubt concerning the adequacy of God's care? Metaphorical image that comes from the earliest biblical narrative comes up against the actuality and particularity of the immediate experience of these people. One becomes aware that sometimes the phrase of affirmation is spoken in a way that conveys liveliness—an affirmation arrived at after genuine engagement of the question. At other times the affirmed confidence seems hollow and the metaphor dead—a mouthing of a pious phrase without power to assure.[16]

My experience with black persons also brings to the fore an awareness that the faithfulness of God as affirmation and as question has about it a note of promise, of something as yet to be finally vindicated as certain. It looks toward something in the future as it reaches toward the deep metaphor coming from the past. To be a child of the covenant therefore means to be a child of God's promises, which are, as we are, still at risk, not yet finalized. The affirmation is grounded finally in hope, not demonstrated certainty.

What of the people who did not have the capacity to retain their integrity in the situation of oppression and poverty? What can be said about the story of their life? First, it would appear that their life story is rooted in the soil of present experience, the social context that immediately surrounds them. Who they are or see themselves to be is determined by what that social situation says to them of its judgments about their worth and dignity. As we say in ordinary speech, they seem to have nothing to fall back on. Theologically speaking, this suggests that human identifications come from two sources: our embeddedness in immediate experience—what Jürgen Moltmann has termed "historical embeddedness"[17]—and our connection to a larger narrative, with its web of meaning that transcends the determinative forces of immediate experience—what for Moltmann is our "eschatological identity." Human identity is for Moltmann therefore always paradoxical, "at the same time" embedded in the historical process of our lives and eschatological in its connection to the narrative of expectation of the coming kingdom. The persons I met who seemed only subject to their immediate social situation can be seen in these terms to have lost their connection to that transcendent identity. Here we encounter again the necessity and priority for Christian pastoral care to help persons to retain that connection with the transcendent.[18]

In turning to consideration of family life in the American sociocultural situation, what "first soundings" by way of theological reflections can we elicit from these data?

What immediately comes to our attention is the tension mentioned earlier between corporate, communal family authority and the press for individuality and self-determination. As we saw, that tension was present both in findings concerning the American family in past centuries and implicitly in the family-system observations of family life in the present. To state that in theological terms, it is a tension between authority and obedience, on the one hand, and individual self-determination on the other. Said another way, it contains the tension between law and individual freedom, commandment and the free exercise of human powers.

If we turn with these theological metaphors toward the biblical narratives that have given reality and form to the metaphors of commandment and law, freedom and obedience, our attention is again drawn to one of the earliest of Old Testament narratives, the story of the covenant community of Israel. That is a story rich with images of commandment and law, the necessity of obedience if the people are to retain their membership in the covenant community. The Mosaic covenant story is not only a story of God's liberation of the people from oppression; it is also the story of God's delineation of what is and is not behavior appropriate to persons who have received the grace of divine liberation. And it is the story of a people who sought self-determination and who often rebelled or went astray from the commandments of Yahweh and followed after their own inclinations. Close examination of the story reveals that its narrative line of development tells of a historical working through of the tension between obedience to law and freedom of self-initiative looking toward that time when "I will put my law within them, and I will write it upon their hearts; and I will be their God, and they shall be my people" (Jer. 31:33). If we who live in another time and place find this age-old tension again working itself out within our families, the work of pastoral care may be enhanced by retrieving from the richness of the biblical narrative some of the images and themes that shaped the plot of that grounding story.

A related theme to that of law and freedom emerges from reflection on the tensions of family life. It has to do with the relationship of the immediate corporate group, the family, to the outside world. Both Greven's Evangelical family and Kantor and Lehr's closed family tend to be self-enclosed. In Greven's understanding, this was important to Evangelicals not only because they tended to distrust the "worldly" surroundings but because it enabled parents better to control the environment in which their children grew to maturity. In the modern context this tendency is more apt to take the form of the family as a unit engaging the outside world and of great parental attention to individual involvements in this world. Issues such as choices of friends, school homework, and vocational decisions are all considered "family business." Intrusions by outside persons, ideas, or activities are often resisted or at least carefully managed.

Greven's Genteel and Kantor and Lehr's random families are much more "worldly" in their orientation. The full exploration of the outside world is encouraged, which means that children of these families are much more subject to the influences of outside groups, value structures, enticements, and the like. Lines of family loyalty are stretched much more thinly and, particularly as the children grow up, may become virtually nonexistent.

Theological reflection prompts the recollection that, from the earliest accounts of the relations of the people of God to the outside world, this issue of withdrawal or involvement with persons and ideas outside the community has been a crucial and sometimes contentious one. From the beginning of the biblical covenant community, the question of the relationship to the stranger and to alien ideas was again and again at issue. The ethicist Joseph L. Allen, in a recent book that develops a covenantal model of Christian ethics, *Love and Conflict,* says that biblical covenant tradition acknowledges two levels of covenant relationship: the inclusive covenant and special covenants. The inclusive covenant expresses God's intention in creation and involves God's relationship (and by implication our human relationship) to all created life. God's faithful care and concern is toward all, both those within the chosen covenant community and those without it.

Special covenants, on the other hand, involve "a relationship of entrusting and accepting entrustment between two or more parties that arises out of some *special* historical transaction between the members, and not only from their participation in the inclusive covenant."[19] Allen goes on to say that we who participate in the covenant community express our loyalty to the inclusive covenant largely through the quality of our special covenants. Where conflicts exist between special covenants and the inclusive covenant, the inclusive covenant should in all cases take precedence.

As the work of this book develops, we shall undertake a more in-depth consideration of the covenant narrative model and its implications for modern life and pastoral care. I have turned to some of the themes of covenant in these preliminary theological reflections deliberately to demonstrate an important truth about theological reflection. Beginning in a situation in the present that raises practical questions, theological reflection not only looks back toward the narrative themes, metaphors, and images from the past that may inform the present situation, it also looks ahead and involves imaginative possibilities for one or another future.[20]

In this chapter I have attempted to open up the notion that the situation in which we find ourselves in the context of modern life with its pluralism and fragmentation sets a high priority on the task of recovering fundamentally Christian modes of interpretation and bringing them to bear on the particularity and diversity of problems of modern living. I have used as case examples both my own memories of ministry with poor black persons caught in the fragmenting forces of racism and published observations of pervasive and long-standing issues of family life. A model for theological reflection concerning present ministry problems has been tentatively introduced that builds upon a general theory of the narrative structure of human experience, with specific attention paid to some of the core narratives of the Judeo-Christian tradition. My stated goal for pastoral care is that of enabling and nurturing Christian life in the modern world.

Having taken these tentative steps toward a narrative hermeneutical re-visioning of pastoral care, let us turn to a more systematic examination of recent work in the field of narrative theology. We will be looking for ways in which that approach to theological thinking can support a narrative hermeneutical theory of pastoral care for the time just ahead in the culture of the West.

2

Stories and *The Story:*
Narrative Theology and the Task
of Pastoral Care

In chapter 1 we made a preliminary foray into developing a narrative mode of understanding the present situation in American cultural life and the peculiar problems it presents for pastoral care ministry. Reflection on two examples of the problem of sustaining a deeply rooted identity in the midst of the pluralism and rapid social change were used to open up some of the possibilities that come into view when seen through the lens of narrative interpretation. Our goal is to find an approach to practical theological thinking that can undergird the pastor's caring response to the stories of human need and conflict heard in the course of pastoral work—stories that express the impact of modern life.

Narrative Theology Described

Before moving on to this specific task, I want to consider more carefully the approach that has come to be called "narrative theology." Like most new or revised emphases in theology, narrative theology has come to mean a number of related but different things. And, as is often the case with new emphases, the term itself has threatened through increasingly popular usage to become simply a slogan. As might be expected also, there are unresolved differences among biblical and theological scholars about the meaning and usage of the term. While it is beyond the scope of this book to sort out all these issues, I would like to clarify the ways in which I am proposing to use a narrative theological approach to pastoral care and also to acknowledge the sources of those ways in the work of others. If pastoral care is to recover its grounding in Christian meanings and Christian

modes of interpretation, that recovery must take place by means
of an undergirding practical theology rooted deeply in Christian
metaphors and meanings.

In a carefully and critically done introduction to narrative
theology, the Jewish theologian Michael Goldberg has developed
a useful typology of approaches to emphasizing biblical narrative
as a source of theological analysis.[1] He calls his typology a
"rough and ready" one, since, as is the case with most typologies,
the placement of particular scholars within one or another type
is somewhat arbitrary. His categories are, however, quite helpful
for us, because they directly relate to the *practical* implications
of their usage. It seems worthwhile, therefore, to summarize the
typology at some length before proceeding to the task of detailing
the ways in which our structure for practical theological thinking
will be grounded in narrative theology.

1. Goldberg's first type "consists of those figures who take the
structure and form of narrative as being the best guide for
understanding the structure of reality." His designation for them
is therefore *structuring the story*. The two persons Goldberg
proposes as best representing this type are Hans Frei[2] and Sallie
McFague.[3]

Frei, whose theological interests have been concerned primarily with the relationship between religious thought and Western
culture, sets for himself the difficult task of critically evaluating
the heavy emphasis in biblical studies during the last two hun-
dred years on scientific modes of determining the "truth" of
biblical texts. One result of that dominance of scientific histori-
ography has been "the separation of a biblical narrative's meaning from its truth and the disjunction between the story and
'reality.' "[4] The result has been the abstraction of the "meanings"
of biblical narratives from their stories and the insertion of these
meanings into other stories thought to depict reality in some
more nearly true or meaningful way.[5] Frei's project then becomes
one of taking with greater seriousness the structural shape of
biblical narrative as the shape of reality.[6] While biblical narratives were not presented in the original situations in which they
were produced as simply chronicles of historic events, they do
have, says Frei, a history-like quality in that they tell of real events
in ways that cause the story to be the meaning so that description
and meaning cohere.[7]

Goldberg's placement of theologian Sallie McFague in the
category he calls "structuring the story" comes from his assessment of her book *Speaking in Parables*. In this book, McFague
analyzes the structure of a particular kind of story, the parable,

and proposes that parables offer the only proper way in which the religious person can speak at one level of historic human events and at the same time speak of the activity of God in history. She says that the Judeo-Christian tradition has spoken on these two levels about historic events not simply by giving surface descriptions in accounts of events but by giving accounts "fraught with background."

> *The only legitimate way of speaking of the incursion of the divine into history, or so it appears to this tradition, is metaphorically.* Metaphor is proper to the subject-matter because God remains hidden. The belief that Jesus is the word of God—that God is manifest somehow in a human life—does not dissipate metaphor but in fact intensifies its centrality, for what is more indirect—a more complete union of the realistic and the strange—than a human life as the abode of the divine? Jesus as the word is metaphor par excellence; he is the parable of God [8]

Thus for McFague the narrative structure of reality, when viewed through the eyes of religious faith, is always fundamentally metaphorical. It is a way of talking about the events of history and of present experience that acknowledges that what one says about events and their meaning both is and is not true to the reality about which one is attempting to speak. It both is and is not true to the facticity of those events. And it both is and is not true to the meaning of the activity of God, for God both is revealed and remains hidden. That is the meaning of metaphor. It always partakes of the is and the is not.[9]

Another important aspect of Sallie McFague's approach to narrative theology concerns her conviction that the parabolic narrative structure of biblical stories is true to the structure of ordinary human life. It "rings true" to the structure of human experience. By this McFague means both what I suggested in chapter 1, concerning the way in which we humans connect the variegated aspects of our lives by means of story, *and* that the transformation of meanings of ordinary experience takes place by means of the formation of new connections of one experience with another in ways in which they had not heretofore been connected. Thus metaphor and parable are not simply confined to biblical ways of speaking of human experience but are present, often in unconscious or hidden ways, in the flow of everyday experience.

It is important to keep in mind that Goldberg's typology is indeed a very rough one since, while both Frei and McFague see narrative as articulating reality, they see it doing so in very different ways. Frei sees biblical narrative in particular as presenting the work of God with God's people at literal, figural, and applicative levels, closely and naturally merged. McFague's interest is in the power of metaphor, especially parable, to throw into crisis the world of our accustomed experience, a feature of biblical as well as other literature. Later in this chapter I will speak in some detail of ways in which the approaches to narrative theology taken by Hans Frei and Sallie McFague undergird the narrative hermeneutical mode of practical theological thinking I am seeking to develop. At this point I only ask that the reader take note of the three most important emphases of this narrative theology type: (1) the narrative structure of human experience, (2) the necessity of narrative metaphorical language for speaking simultaneously of empirically describable human events and of the activity of God in those events, and (3) the relationship between metaphor and transformation of meaning.

2. Michael Goldberg gives his second type of approach to narrative theology the designation *following the story*. The two figures he uses as examples of this type are the Episcopal theologian Paul van Buren[10] and the Jewish scholar Irving Greenberg.[11] Van Buren's principal argument is with the tendency in theological thought to make of God a philosophical abstraction and thus to lose track of the images of the God of the Bible that are fundamentally personal. He advocates a return to the biblical narratives of God's free and personal activity: the God who promises, covenants, limits God's own freedom, takes responsibility for some things but not for others. Thus, by following the stories of God in the Bible, our understanding of God is enlivened and made personally relevant to the issues of life. To do that inevitably means speaking of God as of persons.[12]

As a Jewish scholar of the twentieth century, Irving Greenberg is faced with the necessity of confronting the enormous problem for Jewish theology presented by the Holocaust. He does this by acknowledging what he calls "the statistical norm of human existence" in the untold suffering of millions of people, not only through the Holocaust but by all forms of oppression, poverty, and exploitation. Over against that dismal picture of human possibility, Greenberg sets the story of the exodus. Even though all the evils of the world that existed before the exodus story still exist after it, the exodus story shows "*as history* that the world carries with it the possibility of being fully redeemable in the future."[13] Jewish history is a testimony to that possibility.

This emphasis on following the biblical narrative accounts of the activity of God on behalf of God's people, both in interpretation of present events and in grounding human hopes for the future, is also very important for a narrative hermeneutical approach to pastoral care ministry.

3. Michael Goldberg's third type of emphasis in narrative theology is called *enacting the story.* This type, according to Goldberg, includes those theologians whose primary concern is with the ethic expressed through biblical narrative. Goldberg points to the work of the ethicists Stanley Hauerwas and John Howard Yoder as primary examples of this emphasis in interpretation of biblical narratives. The so-called character ethics of Stanley Hauerwas is of particular significance here. In his book *Vision and Virtue*,[14] Hauerwas takes issue with the tendency in ethical thought to consider ethical problems as problems of "right decision," as if the ethical life were simply a matter of making one right decision after another. He also argues against the so-called "situation ethics" made popular by Joseph Fletcher. Over against both these modes of ethical thinking, which Hauerwas finds to be too "occasional"—that is, too tied to a single occasion and its immediate context of decision—he proposes an ethics of character.

> For the Christian moral life, like any life, is not solely the life of decision. It is also the life of vision—a vision that is determined by the religious and moral notions that constitute it. To be a Christian in effect is learning to see the world in a certain way and thus become as we see. The task of contemporary theological ethics is to state the language of faith in terms of the Christian responsibility to be formed in the likeness of Christ. [15]

For Hauerwas the process of learning to see the world in the way formed in the likeness of Christ is directly related to the appropriation of Christian metaphors and stories. Stories and metaphors suggest ways in which to see and describe the world. They provide for us a narrative structure for interpretation of the ordinary events of our lives. "Stories and metaphors do this by providing the narrative accounts that give our lives coherence."[16]

Here comes into view a way of thinking about the task of pastoral care in the context of communities of faith that is grounded in fundamental ways in narrative theology. Pastoral care may thus be seen as the pastoral facilitation of a process whereby members of the household of God come to see and be formed by the images and themes, metaphors and stories, that shape a Christian vision of the world and of human affairs in the world. Pastoral care finds its purpose in the interpretation of ordinary human affairs in ways that give ordinary life coherence because it is seen as enacting a Christian story.

There remain a number of issues and differences among the three approaches to narrative theology Michael Goldberg has distinguished. Resolution of those issues lies outside the scope of this book. My concern is to mine the rich resources for practical theological interpretation in the work of pastoral care ministry to be found in narrative theology rather than to enter contentiously into the controversies that separate theorists in the field.

Narrative Theology Understanding This Book

Let us now turn to the task of summarizing the ways or "senses" in which a theological understanding of interpretation grounded in narrative is important for the work of practical theological thinking set forth in the chapters that follow. While for purposes of analysis and description these senses will be categorized and listed, it should be kept in mind that they interlock and overlap to form a way of seeing, a way of going about the pastoral interpretive task.

The Bible and history as the "story of God"

This sense in which practical theological thinking is grounded in narrative is, of course, rooted in the faith that the Bible provides us with an overarching narrative in which all other narratives of the world are nested. The Bible is the story of God. The story of the world is first and foremost the story of God's activity in creating, sustaining, and redeeming that world to fulfill God's purposes for it. The story of the world is the story of God's promises for the world. It is also the story of the vicissitudes of God's gracious and creative effort to fulfill those promises, efforts which are in various ways disclosed in the narratives contained in the Bible. Most important of all, the Bible contains the story of God's disclosure and redemptive activity in the coming of Jesus.

The biblical story of God is an open-ended story. It does not stop with the end of the collection of biblical texts. Rather it concerns the activity of God in all of history, a story that continues in the present and is to be fulfilled in the future. The biblical story of God is thus the story of an active, purposing, covenanting, promising, and redeeming God who has always had and continues to have a stake in whatever takes place in God's world. Narrative hermeneutical practical theological thinking must therefore always be firmly rooted in the question of God's praxis, God's activity on behalf of the world.

In relating all of practical theological interpretation to the biblical narrative of God, we must acknowledge the pluralism of stories of God's activity to be found in the Bible. In that rich variety there are a number of themes that interplay and are at times to a considerable extent in tension with each other. The Bible is therefore not a single story of God but rather a series of clusters of stories, each of which both reveals the story of God found in a particular context, and from the particular perspective of the writer or recorder of the story, and allows God to in some sense remain concealed. The language of the biblical stories of God is always in some way metaphorical language. It is metaphorical because that is the only way we humans have of speaking about God. God is both hidden and revealed in human metaphors. One might say that God is both present and absent, in that human narrative metaphors both present God and fall short of revealing God's mystery.[17]

Despite the pluralism of the Bible and the necessity of its metaphorical language, the stories of the Bible taken together disclose a way of seeing the world and human life in the world as always held within the "plot" of God's intentional purposes and direction. Life in the world is life nested within that overarching narrative. One set of organizing themes of that plot involves the human problem of God's otherness from the world and from humans in the world *and* God's active presence—God's silence *and* God's voice of disclosure.[18]

The Bible and history as the story of the people of God

This is the sense in which the history of human life, both at the level of universal human history and that of the history of a particular people, the covenant people of God, is interpreted as a narrative involving all humans in an ongoing relationship with God in all the changing circumstances of history. This vision of human history is likewise rooted in the narratives of the Bible. Those narratives in pluriform ways tell a story of the creation of human life by the gracious act of a loving God as well as the story of the greatness and misery of human actions. They tell the story of human proneness to sin and evil and human possibility for freedom and creative action in the co-creation with God of a future that fulfills both God's purpose and human hopes for abundant life.

This narrative theological sense permeates all aspects of interpretation of humans in relation to time: past, present, and future. The story of the people of God and of all people as formed in the image of God is an ongoing story that gives coherence to these three dimensions of time. By means of the metaphors and images of this narrative the past is given interpretive coherence, so that our understanding involves not simply the chronicling one after another of human events and relationships in time, but rather the interpretive record of human actions as seen through the lenses of biblical metaphors and images. Human history becomes not simply the story of human triumphs and human failures, but rather human faithfulness and unfaithfulness to the grounding narrative that identifies persons as creatures of God. The human experience of the present likewise becomes not simply the impingements and contingency of random events, but rather the present experience of occasions for faithful adherence to the central metaphorical meanings of the grounding story of human identity. The future dimension of time also takes on the interpretive meanings having to do with "following the story," to use Michael Goldberg's phrase. The future provides the possibility of fulfillment of human hopes for the happy outcome to the human story embodied in the vision of that story as the story of the people *of God*.

These first two senses in which I am grounding practical theological thinking in narrative theology are, of course, closely tied to one another because of their base in biblical narratives. The story of God is the story of God who is active in the affairs of the world, most particularly in human affairs. To speak about the affairs of God and the affairs of humans in that manner is to resort to a story of an ongoing relational process moving, by the grace of God and the activity of God's Spirit, toward fulfillment involving both humans and God—indeed, all creation and God— together. But to speak in that manner is, as was said earlier, to speak metaphorically. It is to acknowledge that when we speak of human history, past, present, and future, we speak on two levels, one concrete and empirical, the other metaphorical in that it is a human effort to speak of what is for us ineffable— beyond human capacity to speak about in concrete empirical terms. Like all metaphors, therefore, our metaphors about human history and human future in relation to God always partake of the is and the is not. Any human attempt to collapse those two levels of language into one literal, empirical level results inevitably in idolatry, illusion, and sin.

The narrative structure of human consciousness

In the terms of Michael Goldberg's typology, I am here casting my lot with those who "structure the story." At this point I need, however, to express my dissatisfaction with Goldberg's turn of the phrase. It is more accurate to say that the story structures reality rather than that the story is structured. For at a fundamental level of assertion about human experience this is a philosophical/theological/psychological judgment about the way humans structure life embedded in time. Because time passes moment by moment, and because of the human capacity to transcend time through memory and anticipation, we humans structure life in time in terms of narrative. It is not therefore simply fortuitous that the Bible—and, indeed, all human recording of events and anticipation of future events—is in the form of narrative. Narrative structures the human experience of life in time. "To put it another way, *time becomes human to the extent that it is articulated through a narrative mode, and narrative attains its full meaning when it becomes a condition of temporal existence.*"[19]

This quotation from Paul Ricoeur locates the notion of story as the human structure of time philosophically within the existentialist/phenomenological tradition that goes back to Edmund Husserl, Wilhelm Dilthey, and Martin Heidegger. It is this tradition within which the modern discipline of philosophical hermeneutics developed.[20] Ricoeur further clarifies the narrative structure of the human experience of time in the following way:

> By saying that there is not a future time, a past time, and a present time, but a threefold present, a present of future things, a present of past things, and a present of present things, Augustine set us on the path of an investigation into the most primitive temporal structure of action. It is easy to rewrite each of the three temporal structures of action in terms of this threefold present. The present of the future? *Henceforth,* that is, from now on, I commit myself to doing that *tomorrow.* The present of the past? *Now* I intend to do that because I *just* realized that. . . . The present of the present? *Now* I am doing it, because *now* I can do it. The actual present of doing something bears witness to the potential present of the capacity to do something and is constituted as the present of the present. . . . What counts here is the way in which everyday praxis orders the present of the future, the present of the past, and the present of the present in terms of one another. For it is this practical articulation that constitutes the most elementary inductor of narrative.[21]

This phenomenology of the human experience of time, as Ricoeur has formulated it, will be very important in the structure for practical theological thinking to be developed in the next chapter. Because of its human narrative structure, human praxis

brings past, present, and future together into play in the interpretation and decision making that make up human response to
any present situation in time. So praxis—and, most particularly,
practical theological thinking in the situation of praxis—always
involves an essentially narrative structure.

The human structuring of time as narrative can be validated
psychologically as well as philosophically. In my earlier book,
The Living Human Document, I wrote extensively about that,
using some of the recent developments in psychoanalytic ego
psychology and object relations theory.[22] There is psychological
evidence for the notion that from a very early age, perhaps as
early as infancy, humans begin to structure mythical stories of
the self and of the world, most particularly the world of significant relationships. By means of stories of the self and of the world
around us we hold together events, persons, and experiences that
would otherwise be fragmented. To be a person is therefore to
live in a story.

The individual story of the self is not, however, constructed in
a vacuum. Rather, that story is both located within a series of
larger human stories and draws its images and themes, its metaphors and evaluative ideas, from those larger stories. So when I
speak of the human structuring of time as narrative, I am speaking both of individual human consciousness and of corporate
modes of living within time and living out a narrative of what it
is to live in time. The study of these larger narratives is what is
involved in the study of culture and ethos, both at the level of
local geographical location and at the level of the great cultures
of the world.

The understanding of human consciousness as structured in
narrative is, however, not simply an understanding at philosophical, psychological, and cultural levels. It is an understanding
that is also grounded theologically in the deeply rooted biblical
understanding of God as a God of history who created the world
and set it in time. The narratives of creation are set in time, and
the crowning act of creation as described in those narratives was
the act of the creation of humans as creatures of time. So at the
deepest theological level, human experience is structured in
time and narrative.

The pluralism of narratives

As I have indicated, the term *narrative theology* implies that
the interpretation of the affairs of the world by Christian theology
is fundamentally metaphorical. It both is and is not a complete

and full interpretation. As such, Christian theology represents one story among many possible stories (or, more accurately, a cluster of stories among many possible clusters of stories) of the affairs of the world. The Judeo-Christian story stands alongside other stories concerning the affairs of the world and, particularly in the situation of modernity discussed in chapter 1, must be kept alive and viable in relation to those other narratives. There is therefore a continuing necessity to reinterpret the meanings of the Judeo-Christian narrative and its metaphors, a necessity created in part by the continuing emergence of other ways of seeing the affairs of the world.

This constantly shifting scene involving the pluralism of narratives means that the Judeo-Christian story must be critically appropriated and reappropriated in relation to other religious stories: Buddhism, Islam, and the other great religions of the world. Equally, if not more importantly, however, in an age of secularism, the Judeo-Christian story must be critically appropriated and reinterpreted in relation to the stories of human affairs implicit in the scientific/technological ways of speaking about the affairs of the world that have become dominant in Western culture.

The notion that even scientific/technological ways of speaking about the affairs of the world express an undergirding narrative about the world may seem strange and disconnected from the language commonly used by physical and social scientists. It simply means that whenever a scientist of whatever scientific discipline sets out to establish a scientific principle or research an area or some phenomenon of interest, he or she takes along a whole set of assumptions into that scientific project—assumptions that have within them, at least implicitly, a narrative or story about how and why things happen as they do. The scientist, in moving from the known to the unknown, does so by means of analogy or the projection of a narrative about what is known into the context of the unknown. To be sure, the scientist (as, incidentally, the theologian) quickly moves in some way to objectify or abstract from that narrative into whatever set of symbols, concepts, designations, or word labels are appropriate in order to be able to manipulate, examine, or verify those abstractions. But beneath or standing behind the abstractions is some essentially narrative understanding of the world and its affairs.

It is important for the work of practical theology that we use to advantage the manner in which other ways of speaking about the affairs of the world each provide an "angle of vision," or perspective, on the story of the world and human affairs in the world. Each angle of vision provides a more or less different form of illumination from that of the theological angle of vision contained in the Christian narrative. To be responsible (using the word *responsible* in H. Richard Niebuhr's sense of the term) in the continuing process of critical reinterpretation and reappropriation of the Judeo-Christian story means bringing that story and its metaphors into dialogue with those of other ways of seeing the world. That means to engage at many levels of sophistication and analysis in what I will call in the next chapter, following the Catholic theologian David Tracy, the method of mutually critical correlation. To engage in mutually critical correlation means to correlate in a relatively even-handed fashion the metaphors and themes of the Judeo-Christian story with the insights and perspectives of other ways of constructing the story of the world and its affairs.

To be a responsible practical theologian in the modern pluralistic context means then that the pastor must, insofar as time, knowledge, and skill permit, be prepared to be multidisciplinary in orientation and practice. Practical theology is thereby appropriately a generalist discipline that draws freely upon the specialized knowledge of many different, more narrowly structured perspectives and ways of accumulating knowledge about the world. That appropriation of specialized knowledge must, however, be a disciplined appropriation that is itself shaped by the process of mutually critical correlation which tests the perspectives of other narratives by their abrasion against the Christian narrative, even as that narrative is itself tested and reinterpreted.

Narrative theology and the transformation of life

Practical narrative theology is, then, the careful and critical effort to bring into some coherent pattern all four of the foregoing senses of narrative theology in the process of bringing them to bear on any practical situation of ministry. Narrative practical theology is, therefore, an ongoing hermeneutical process within the immediate storied context of ministry. The intention of that process is the transformation of the human story, both individual and corporate, in ways that open the future of that story to creative possibilities. By faith that means nesting the individual and corporate human story finally within the biblically grounded narrative of the God who is both transcendent of the human story (God's "otherness") and active within that ongoing story (God's suffering, gracious, redemptive "presence").

Thus the notion of transformation as the purpose of narrative practical theology functions at two levels. First, it functions at the level of the formation of a vision of human transformation from the human side in terms of intentions and practical actions designed to bring about creative transformation. Through mission and ministry, we who are the people of God seek to act to transform human suffering into human health, human injustice into the ways of justice, human sin and failure into human experiences of forgiveness and reconciliation. Practical theological thinking is therefore always directed toward practical transformative human action, and our thinking is tested and given significance by the results of our actions.

But the notion of transformation also functions at a second level, that of human openness and response to the ongoing transformative activity of God. Here, as earlier, the thought of H. Richard Niebuhr is most illuminating. In an article in *The Christian Century* written during World War II, Niebuhr said that "it is a sign of returning health when God rather than the self or the enemy is seen to be the central figure in the great tragedy of war and when the question 'What must I do?' is preceded by the question 'What is God doing?' To attend to God's action is to be on the way to that constructive understanding and constructive human reaction which the prophets initiated."[23]

Generalizing on that affirmation of the primacy of God's transformative action, we are confronted with the necessity in narrative practical theological thinking always to keep an openness to God's present activity in the forefront of our interpretation of situations and of our envisioning of our own human response to situations. According to the grounding narrative of Christian faith, it is in that mysterious transformation that we can finally have confidence. Our speaking about it may of necessity always be metaphorical, and our perception of it as through an unclear glass, but God's praxis is for us the ground of our hope of transformation.

The Role of Faith Narrative in Everyday Life

Before turning to the formulation of a structure for narrative hermeneutical practical theological thinking in the next chapter, it is important to take up the question as to how narrative faith comes to be appropriated in the everyday circumstances of living. The importance of this question is directly related both to the task of pastoral interpretation in concrete situations and to the matter of facilitation of transformation of life by the reappropriation of narrative faith. Though they interrelate in significant ways, there are four primary ways in which a narrative faith is appropriated and made indigenous to the experience of living in the world.

First, and perhaps most commonly, faith in a given narrative of the world and human affairs in the world is appropriated simply by a process of enculturation. As persons grow up in families and in communities shaped by a given cultural ethos they simply pick up in the atmosphere of those various corporate contexts the metaphors and images, the themes and evaluative notions, yes, even the attitudes and feelings that are associated with the story of that ethos. As persons grow up they learn to be humans in that cultural climate as fish learn to swim in the sea.[24] The meanings and metaphors of the ethos come to be taken for granted as the way things are. A "world" of meaning is absorbed and given particular shape by the individual's or the group's experience of it. Here, of course, all that was said in chapter 1 concerning the drastically altered situation of modernity is relevant. Clarity and unity of cultural vision, the oneness of a cultural ethos, is no longer reinforced on every side and in every exposure to contextual influence. But the fact remains that for most persons the first introduction to and immersion in a story of the world comes about through the enculturation that goes on in family, church, and school.

Second, and certainly related to the first, a particular form of narrative faith is appropriated by a process in which the metaphors of the faith narrative are found to have a certain "fit" to something significant that is experienced in the ongoing ebb and flow of everyday life. We experience something of importance to us and connect that experience to some metaphorical meaning, and we say to ourselves in some way, "Oh, that's the way it is!" That is the meaning of what has happened or what I felt or thought.

H. Richard Niebuhr speaks of such moments as moments of revelation. They are moments that create for us what he calls a history "from the inside." Experience is connected with meaning so that the story of our lives is given a certain cast of meaning, a certain mode of metaphorical connection.

> When we speak of revelation we mean that something has happened to us in our history which conditions all our thinking and that through this happening we are enabled to apprehend what we are, what we are suffering and doing and what our potentialities are. What is otherwise arbitrary and dumb fact becomes related, intelligible and eloquent fact through the revelatory event.[25]

Niebuhr does not stop there in his understanding of the revelatory experience. He goes on to say that whatever has happened "compels our faith and . . . requires us to seek rationality and unity in the whole of our history."[26] The "fit" of the connection that has been made between faith and experience must be tested to see if it continues to fit and provides the coherence to life that we need. Furthermore, the "fit" of the connection does not ordinarily take place in isolation from a communal setting within which the person experiences it. As James Gustafson rightly says, not many persons begin the process of connecting interpretation and experience *de novo.* Rather, we are virtually always held within and nourished by communities "which provide interpretations of human experiences, and interpretations of the transcendent, the Holy, which is the object that evokes human response."[27]

Third, we appropriate a faith narrative when the metaphors of that narrative become powerfully disclosive for us in interpreting the events and circumstances, relationships, and values involved in a situation *that requires our human decision and action.* This time of appropriation is often closely related to the second, but it deserves separate designation because of the quality of urgency of choice and active response. It is the time of revelation colored by the insight, *"This* I must do!" It is the moment that tells us that because we live in a world made coherent by *this* narrative, our agency in the situation must be given a certain thrust, a certain direction of intention, a certain goal. In such a moment interpretation and action become one; we become our interpretation.

It is important to acknowledge that such moments of decision and action as those of which I here speak are fraught with both the possibility of right interpretation and with misinterpretation, both good and evil outcome. Most often, in fact, our interpretations in moments of decision and action will partake of both good and evil, both right response to the future envisioned in the narrative and wrongheaded or distorted response. That is the way it is with us. At least that is the way it is with us according to the grounding narrative of Christian faith.

Fourth, we appropriate a faith narrative in moments when the question "What is God doing?" becomes real for us. This is the time of revelation discussed earlier under the rubric of transformation. These are therefore moments when we become profoundly aware of the need of transformation of life, if life as we most deeply desire it is to move ahead. Often they are moments when we experience most profoundly our inability to bring about that desired transformation. The way ahead seems blocked or cloudy. Then perchance (not always, but sometimes) we are enabled to see, as did H. Richard Niebuhr in the situation of world war, the possibility that in the very confluence of events and forces at work in our situation, God may be active and by the power of God's Spirit the situation may be transformed and the way ahead be opened.

In this chapter I have sought to open for the reader the rich resources to be tapped for practical theological thinking in narrative theology. The mode of opening up these resources has itself been hermeneutical, a process of interpretation. It is now time to turn to the task of structuring a methodology for practical theological thinking which utilizes the hermeneutical approach to these resources. If such a narrative practical theology can be constructed and made viable in relation to concrete situations encountered in pastoral care, pastoral work may again be undergirded by the recovery of Christian modes of interpretation.

3

The Structure:
Elements of a Hermeneutical
Theory of Practical Theology

The task of this chapter is to formulate a structure for doing theological reflection in whatever practical situation we may find ourselves in pastoral ministry. The perspective from which I approach the task reflects a certain practical necessity and concern shaped by observations of our present situation to which I have alluded in chapter 1. That perspective, in ways that were discussed at some length in chapter 2, values particularly the possibilities for understanding any human activity by seeing it as grounded in some narrative or story of the way things are and ought to be in the world and thus as an expression of a certain way of seeing and interpreting whatever is going on or at hand. Thus the approach to doing practical theology to be considered is best termed a narrative hermeneutical theory of practical theology, since it takes with utmost seriousness both the connection between human interpretation and action and the reality that all human processes and activities take place in the flow of time, a flow we humans hold in meaningful movement by means of a narrative or storied structure.[1]

A Definition of Practical Theology

Our tentative definition of practical theology will itself suggest a schematization of the situation within which practical theological thinking takes place and a preliminary schematization of the movement of practical theological reflection. Some of the key elements in that movement will need to be further explained before a more comprehensive and theological schema for a practical hermeneutical reflective process can be constructed. What we shall be doing is complex and difficult. The hoped-for rewards are greater clarity and precision concerning a process of practical theological thinking which can result in actions on the part of the people of God that are responsive to the present reality of human needs.

My colleague at Emory University James Fowler, in an essay titled "Practical Theology and the Shaping of Christian Lives," defines practical theology as "critical and constructive reflection on the praxis of the Christian community's life and work in its various dimensions."[2] Fowler moves from this definition quickly to acknowledge that practical theology does not go on independently of other aspects of the theological enterprise, nor is it done in self-sufficient isolation from the so-called secular disciplines that provide hermeneutical perspectives on social and personal experience. Practical theology is therefore inherently interdisciplinary and multilingual in its activity, while yet keeping its grounding identity in the discipline and language of theological thinking.

My definition of practical theology is closely related to that of my colleague and in a sense builds upon it. Like Fowler, I see practical theology as emerging from Christian praxis, but I want to emphasize perhaps more strongly than he that the work of practical theology always takes place in the midst of praxis and is prompted by that situation of "being in the midst." Practical considerations and issues always come first—indeed, they prompt the necessity of practical theological thinking. In that sense practical theology is always, or virtually always, done "on the run," so to speak, or in the midst of the necessity of action. Said another way, practical theology is always "in process," never finalized. To be sure, we may back off, in order to get our reflective bearings and put things in perspective, but even here there must be attention to movement and the necessity of action. The problem becomes one of how to achieve some distance from the problem at hand in order that our actions may be informed by both a broad range of knowledge and a certain quality of objectivity, while yet keeping the situation in which we are required to act within the constraints of time clearly in view. Nowhere in the work of ministry is this situation of having to reflect while under the necessity to act in response more characteristically the case than in the ministry of pastoral care, for, as all pastors know, in pastoral care we are most often required to think critically about what we are doing while in the midst of an ongoing conversation with persons in stress.

A second expansion or elaboration of James Fowler's definition that I wish to make is perhaps implied in his phrase, "community's life and work in its various dimensions." I wish to underline the significance and importance of the widely varying contextual arenas or "action perspectives" that make up the Christian community's life and work. Among the contextual arenas and action perspectives that must be considered are included at least those of professional pastoral context and perspective, the context and action perspective of the gathered or identified Christian community, and the many and varied contexts and action perspectives of the various individual members of that community in their separate vocations and places in the world. This last set of contexts and action perspectives might be thought of as the "dispersed Christian community."

Practical theology, as here conceived, is the critical and constructive reflection on the life and work of Christians in all the varied contexts in which that life takes place with the intention of facilitating transformation of life in all its dimensions in accordance with the Christian gospel. Practical theology, seen from a narrative hermeneutical perspective, involves a process of the interpretive fusion of horizons of meaning embodied in the Christian narrative with other horizons that inform and shape perceptions in the various arenas of activity in which Christians participate.[3]

Behind this definition lie several component ideas, most of which I have already spoken about or implied. It may be useful to list them here in summary form, however.

1. The critical and constructive reflection that makes up the work of practical theology involves reflection on both the horizon of meaning and purpose preserved and transmitted to Christians in the biblical narrative and its component stories, metaphorical images, and themes *and* on the various horizons of meaning that inform and shape modern life in all its arenas and contexts of activity. There is therefore involved a constant mutually critical correlation of perspectives and an effort to bring into fusion the horizon of the Christian interpretation of the world and whatever other horizons are present in the contextual activity.[4] The human effort to bring differing horizons into some fusion that can inform and shape decisions and actions so that what one thinks coheres with what one does is often fraught with considerable conflict and difficulty. The fusion of horizons of meaning rarely involves a simple synthesis of perspectives. More often horizons conflict, even contradict each other. The "world of meaning" shaped by each horizon is challenged and tested by the images and themes, imperatives and assumptions of the other "worlds of meaning." The desire for coherence and fusion is

confronted by the pluralism and contradiction of interpretations. In the crucible of mutual criticism and search for a way of seeing that makes sense, a new and more comprehensive way of seeing the activity under consideration may emerge, though seldom are all the conflicts of differing perspectives resolved. To the degree that a fusion of horizons does take place, a new way of seeing— a lens through which the situation can now be seen—takes form.

At an everyday level, this means that the work of practical theology goes on whenever and wherever persons who consider themselves to be Christians are seeking to bring together their Christian self-understanding and the varied roles, activities, and relationships in which they participate, all of which involve some ideas, images, and meanings of who they are and should be. Whatever the activity, be it a job on an industrial assembly line, the keeping of a house and the parenting of children, participating in a volunteer association, or paying one's taxes, that activity embodies some horizon of meaning concerning human individual and corporate life. Practical theology is being done whenever one or another of those horizons of meaning is being critically correlated with the horizon of the Christian story. It may go on in an individual's private questioning and ruminating thought about who that individual is and what she or he is doing. It may go on in a family dinner conversation about some activity of its members. It will perhaps more formally go on when Christians gather in worship or group discussion of what it means to be members of the people called the people of God. It can and should go on in carefully disciplined ways when pastors and others are engaged in reflection on a social problem confronting the Christian community, the problems and tasks of ministry, or the mission of the church. But wherever and whenever it goes on, it involves an effort to make sense of an activity by means of the symbolic images and themes, yes, even the feelings and unverbalized aspirations that are associated either positively or negatively with the story of Christian experience. Thus, critical reflection on the Christian narrative meanings may never be considered to go on in a vacuum or in a situation separated from the involvements of Christians in the widely varying activities of life in the world. Acknowledged or unrecognized, any reflection on the Christian story is always done vis-à-vis some human contextual activity.

2. The notion that practical theological thinking consists in the fusion of horizons of meaning implies not only utmost respect for the horizon embodied in the Christian story, but also respect for other horizons, other ways of seeing the world and its human

activity. Respect for other horizons necessitates taking care to allow the language symbols and metaphors of those horizons to speak for themselves, to ask the questions which those languages express most directly and clearly, to express the truth that they reveal.

Thus the process of fusion of horizons may be seen as analogous to a conversation between persons who hold differing points of view but who also have some viewpoints in common. At times the conversation will be easy and cordial, each partner seeking both to understand the other and to express the particularity of a given perspective in ways that invite rapprochement. Each seeks to illuminate the other by viewing the matter at hand from the standpoint of a somewhat different world of meaning. As in all conversations, however, there will develop issues to be contested which in the process test both the horizon of Christian understanding and that of other perspectives on the world. The work of practical theology is therefore not always done in the comfortable atmosphere of reflection and easy conversation. Emotions will be stirred and vested interests brought to light. This is true whether the work is being done in a group context, where differing horizons are being strongly represented by various group members, or in the agonizing privacy of individual self-questioning.

The effort to move toward rapprochement and fusion will not, to be sure, always be successful. Some horizons simply stand in stark contradiction or are fundamentally over against each other. Here lie both the possibility of conversion—the more or less radical shifting of fundamental loyalty from one meaning horizon to another—and the possibility of refusal and rejection of one horizon by another.

Viewed from a sociological perspective, I am here of course pointing to the situation of pluralism and the questions it inevitably raises for persons whose identity has been shaped by an appropriation of Christian images of what life is and is meant to be. Pluralism forces interaction and conflict of interpretations of life. The necessity of some vague and ill-defined fusion of the Christian perspective with other ways of seeing the world becomes more urgent and difficult in such a pluralistic cultural context.

In theological terms, this respect for horizons of meaning other than the specifically Christian one is rooted in the work of H. Richard Niebuhr to which I referred in the Introduction. For Niebuhr, responsible Christian interpretation and action always involve response to the other in light of the possibility that through the action of the other upon me God may be acting upon me. I must respond therefore as to the action of God.

3. The fusion of horizons notion also implies a certain "hermeneutic of suspicion" concerning all horizons of understanding, including our own appropriation of the Christian horizon.[5] The dialogical conversation between horizons will reveal blind spots, open unasked questions, compare differing ways of seeing, and in general call into question accustomed ways of interpreting human activity and experience. A hermeneutic of suspicion will also assert the necessity of taking into account the reality that there is more involved in the shaping of human reaction and response to situations in life than the formation of meaning and interpretations of events and relationships. The hard and external forces of occurrence of events, economic necessity, coercion, and the like, as well as the internal forces of psychological dynamics and experienced relational necessity often skew the way situations under consideration are given meaning.[6]

4. Already implied in the first three elements of this definition of practical theology is a fourth, which, because of its central importance, deserves to be considered separately. The purpose of practical theological thinking is always the facilitation of the transformation of life.

At one level our definition implies the transformation of life simply because the story of human life is embedded in the structure of time. Time itself implies change and transformation, because time itself is movement. Life does not stand still but is always in process. Structures of human meaning are therefore always under the necessity of change, always in movement toward an unknown future.

At another level, this is, of course, an element that is itself rooted in the Christian narrative of the world. Life as we experience it within that story of the world is life in need of transformation. Throughout the history of its telling and retelling, even in the time of the Old Testament, the Christian story was a story of human life in need of and awaiting transformation. Not only is this true because all things human are, according to that story, in some way involved in sin and the need of redemption. It is also true because, according to that story, God is still engaged in the creative process of bringing about the rule of God's kingdom in all aspects of created life. The Christian story is therefore a story of God's promise and the transformation of life in accordance with that promise. Paradoxically, the promise of God is, for us, always involved in an "already" and a "not yet." The promise has been fulfilled and is yet to be fulfilled. Short of the final transformation of life in accordance with the kingdom of God, the human story is seen as one in which there is a persistent involvement of humans in injustice, distortion of the purpose of life, and errors in both interpretation and action, both self-understanding and relationships.

This element in the definition implies that the truth of the gospel emerges and is tested in the crucible of the fusion of horizons of human understanding. By that process the metaphors and images of the gospel are constantly kept alive and are themselves subject to transformation of meaning in relation to human life in the world. Like the human appropriation of any horizon of meaning, our appropriation of the Christian horizon tends to become fixed and stagnant. Thereby its ability to provide interpretive guidance for persons called Christian in the ever-changing and pluralistic arenas of human activity becomes limited and closed to the new activity of God in the power of the Spirit. Only as the process of practical theological thinking is kept open and active, alive in dialogue with other perspectives on reality, can the Christian community remain open to the movement of God that, according to our grounding Christian story, may be found taking place in the darkest corners of arenas far afield from our accustomed Christian contexts.

A Schematic Structure
for Narrative Practical Theological Thinking

Our definition of practical theology, together with the elements already outlined, implies an informal but definite and ordered process whereby careful theological reflection can best be carried out. It is a process grounded in the human narrative ordering of time as past, present, and future. I have come to think of this structure schematized in the form of a double loop and then a series of reflective feedback loops in some such fashion as in Figure 1.

This schema suggests that carefully structured practical theological thinking involves a movement from reflection on the present activity and our human experience of it—with whatever pain and conflict that may involve—toward reflection on the "story" of how that activity came to be structured as it is, the meanings and interpretations that shaped the activity. Our reflection dips into the past in search of causal connections, traditions of meaning, and taken-for-granted roles and relationships. Our search is for the root of the horizon of understanding that informs the human activity. Here we may make use of whatever language and analysis tools are available to us from a variety of disciplines and customs, practical wisdom, and the like, associated with the activity under consideration. At a sophisticated theoretical level the analysis of origins of a particular horizon informing an activity will involve careful interdisciplinary correlation of differing first principles, methodologies, and languages. In most ordinary situations encountered in everyday life, however, these differing principles, methodologies, and languages will more often remain in the background while reflection on their derivatives are in the foreground of reflection and/or interpersonal interaction.

**The Given or Implied Narrative Structure of the
Human Activity Under Consideration**

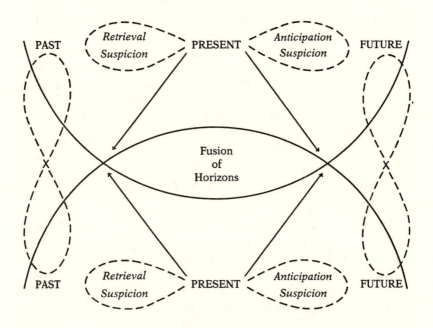

The Narrative Structure of Christian Understanding
of Human Activity

Figure 1. A structure for narrative practical theological thinking.

With our enlarged understanding of the past history of the human activity before us, we then move back through the present toward a search for the intended future embodied in the activity and its history. Toward what ends does this human activity take us? What outcomes are implicit in the way the activity has been and is being carried out?

Returning to the present situation in the human activity at hand, we now are able to see that activity more clearly in the light of its narrative, its lived story. The horizon of meaning implicit in the activity is more vividly before us.

The schema suggests a similar structure of reflection in relation to the Christian narrative of the world and the implications of that narrative for human activity. Again, the movement is from our present appropriation of that narrative (with whatever pain and conflict may be involved) toward the past, perhaps most particularly toward those biblical narrative metaphors, themes, images, and assessments of human activity from which our appropriation of the Christian story originated. It also, however, may involve a movement into the past history of our own and our more immediate predecessors' appropriation of the Christian story.

Our movement into the past in relation to the Christian narrative will always, as in the case of the human activity being considered, prompt us to move toward the future. What is the Christian vision for the human future? How is that future to be brought into reality? What is required of us as Christians if we are to be in harmony with the future God is bringing about?

The schematic diagram suggests that, if we are not to be unwittingly caught up in false consciousness and illusion as we both seek to retrieve the meanings of the past and anticipate the meanings for the future contained in the plot, either of the story of the human activity under consideration or of the Christian story, a healthy hermeneutic of suspicion needs to be at work. We need always to be questioning our assumed meanings, our easily arrived at connections and conclusions. Practical theological thinking at this level requires a healthy lacing of skepticism about our own prejudices.

In the schema here envisioned, another inevitability takes place. The two narrative structures, that of the human activity about which we seek greater clarity and that of the Christian story, begin to feed back upon one another. Here is the process David Tracy has called mutually critical correlations. In the language I have been using taken from Hans-Georg Gadamer, the two horizons of the two narratives begin to fuse with one another, with the result that both are subject to transformation. The truth of the Gospel story impacts the interpreted human reality of the activity. In that mutual abrasion the movement of both our appropriation of the Christian story through time and of human activity is broken open and made vulnerable to reinterpreted meaning and transformed activity.

The schematization I have given suggests a far more formal and scheduled process than is usually the case in the actual situations in which practical theological thinking is done. In practice the process is much more informal and unstructured. It may be only the occurrence of an agonizing question about some activity or relationship, expressed in private thought as "How did I get in this situation?" "What is going on here?" "Is this really where I want to be?" or "Is this really what I want to do?" A connection may be made with some aspect of the person's Christian self-understanding. "Here I have always thought of myself as a Christian and I am doing this?" The "story" being lived out in the activity does not comport with the envisioned "story" of the self as connected to the Christian story. Or practical theological thinking may go on informally among persons involved in a common task or caught in the same situation. But it should also be kept in mind that it is central to the mission and ministry of the church both to equip persons for doing practical theological thinking in relation to all activities of life and to provide occasions with both individuals and groups when practical theological thinking may take place in a more disciplined and careful fashion. This means, of course, that not only must pastors be able to do disciplined practical theological thinking themselves, they must also be prepared to engage their parishioners in formal and informal ways which nurture the capacity in them.

The Multidimensional Nature of Practical Theology

Elaborate as my schematization may seem, it does not yet take into account the important consideration that all human activity is multidimensional and involves persons in integrating multiple roles and multiple action perspectives. Thus any practical theological thinking concerning a single human activity needs always to relate that activity to all others in which individuals and groups are involved and to the multiplicity of stories of past, present, and future in which human activity takes place. Not only that, but multiple roles generate multiple standpoints from which to view any activity. Seen from the perspective of one standpoint, the activity takes on an appearance governed by the "place" or role standpoint from which one is looking. So practical theological thinking virtually always involves setting a priority of significance for one or another "angle of vision" over against others, while yet taking others into consideration.

Although practical theology is a mode of thinking engaged in to some extent by all persons who think of themselves as Christians and not simply by pastors, I want now to consider the matter of multiple role perspectives as it impinges on the parish pastor's work in practical theology, as illustration and also to demonstrate how a pluralism of perspectives complicates practical theological thinking. This occurs within the community of Christians itself and for the pastor as leader of such a community. When some larger arena of public life is considered, the problem is still further complicated.

The multiple roles and perspectives from which the parish pastor must view the life and work of a local congregation, are schematized in Figure 2.

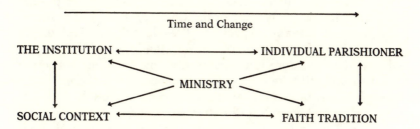

Figure 2. The multiple roles and perspectives of the pastor.

Each corner represents an area of responsibility and interest to which the parish pastor must attend. The pastor is in some respects the administrator of an institution, the local church. Such matters as budget, building, membership cultivation, stewardship, and the like must be given both attention and leadership. In our pattern of social reality, the community of faith is lodged in the institutional church. From that perspective, the whole of the pastor's role—indeed, the whole of Christian life in the world—will tend to look a certain way. Agendas for activity, priorities in regard to decisions and choices, relationships to persons inside and outside the institutional church, and a multitude of other considerations and concerns will emerge from that role relationship and its perspective on the whole of things.

But pastors are also called to be pastoral shepherds in relationship to members of the community of faith as individuals. That means, among other things, that the pastor needs to be attentive to the individual parishioner's perspective on all aspects of life, not only within the community of faith but also in the larger life situation. From that viewpoint the realities of church as institution—indeed, all the realities of life itself—will present a very different appearance. Even among parishioners there will exist a multitude of differing perspectives on life together as Christians and on life in the world. To all these differing viewpoints and ways of experiencing life in relation to Christian faith the pastor must attend, inviting sharing and reflection.

In the lower left-hand corner are located the perspectives on the life and work of the church and its mission that comes from giving attention to the larger social situation in which the church finds itself in a given time and place. Issues that are present in the larger community set missional priorities as they demand responses from the people of God. Forces at work in the larger social situation impinge upon what is possible for both the church as a community and individuals within the community.

The lower right-hand corner of the figure signifies the pastor's responsibility as interpreter of the Christian faith and tradition. The pastor is in many respects the "resident theologian" for the community of faith. As seen from the standpoint of that responsibility, the considerations represented by the other corners of the diagram will take on a particular appearance shaped by the metaphorical images and themes, normative models, and affirmations embodied in the Christian story and tradition.

Figure 2 underlines the tension that exists among all these perspectival standpoints. Pastors must be able to place themselves in any one of these locations and see the situation or activity at hand as from that standpoint. Indeed, the pastor must be able to act in a variety of situations from the standpoint of each or, more often, in the tension among the several perspectives. To do this with grace and skill requires not only practical theological thinking but the ability to balance demands and communicate a certain practical wisdom and judgment.

The difficulty involved in such a multidimensional relationship is inherent in the role of the pastor as facilitator of the interpretive process of the fusion of horizons of understanding. Horizons of understanding not only have developed out of a history of embeddedness in a sociocultural process, they also grow out of location. Pastors who are sensitive to differing perspectives coming from differing locations will not stay in any one posture for long at a time. Rather they will move from one location to another (i.e., different corners of the diagram) in response to the need for another angle of vision. The intention will be to see that an unattended perspective is heard, an unrecognized consideration is taken into account.

Here the image of the pastor as interpretive guide and mediator in relation both to the faith tradition and the human situation seems significant as an organizing tool. This involves the pastor placing himself or herself in the midst of the tension of perspectives, seeking to mediate them. It is a locating of the pastoral self with the hope and expectation that the fusion of horizons of perspectives will bring into focus a truly new and shared understanding, a more openly shared praxis of the Christian life on the part of all persons and points of view involved. That, to be sure, can be a most uncomfortable place in which to locate oneself. Yet it seems inherent in the pastoral role, given the unavoidable, even at times redemptive, situation of the conflict of interpretations. It requires the pastor's genuine respect for differing perspectives. It also requires the pastor's confidence that pressures and constraints from conflicting forces inherent in the situation can be overcome and even used to reach a new understanding.

Yet another tension with which every pastor must live and take account of in the day-to-day work of practical theology is the tension between what is ideally called for and what, given the realities of the concrete situation, is possible—the tension between the "is" and the "ought."[7] The pastor needs both a vision of what might be—what, indeed, in the light of the coming kingdom, we are called to become—and a realistic sense of what, given human finite limitation *and* the human penchant for sin and error, it is possible to do. Without some ability to balance those two considerations, the pastor will find her or his efforts ending in either the frustration of unrealized hopes or the cynicism of despair.

Human Praxis and the Praxis of God

It is of crucial importance to ground pastoral identity in the narrative images and metaphors of the Christian story. The task of mediating perspectives that are inherently in tension can almost literally pull the pastor apart or bring about a futile effort to serve many masters. Resisting that loss of the integrity of one's commitment to the task of representing the Christian vision of reality involves entrusting one's identity and the outcomes of one's efforts to the mysterious working out of the story of God's "praxis," God's activity in and through our activity.

This theological notion that our activities are permeated and given redemptive coherence and direction by the activity of God is a central theme of the Christian story. In a sense, it grounds all other themes of that story; it is what it means to be the people *of* God. In narrative language, it is the central plot. God's covenant with Israel which began the long story of the people of God was a covenant of promise that in whatever circumstance God's activity on human behalf would not be taken away. In return, human activity involves placing that activity within a structure of response to the activity of God. Seen hermeneutically, our human interpretations are to be made in the light of an expectation of God's redemptive action. Our actions are enfolded within and look for their fulfillment and redemption through the actions of God.

A more comprehensive schema for maintaining a formative connection between our interpretations of human situations requiring our action (the carrying forward of our stories) and our appropriation of the ongoing Christian story of God's action will facilitate the process of our praxis (practice of life) becoming Christian praxis.

Figure 3 schematizes several important things concerning practical theological thinking, when it is undertaken *both* as a process of hermeneutical retrieval of the Christian tradition and its narrative images and themes *and* within an attitude of openness to the present and future redemptive and transformative activity of God.

We have no alternative but to begin with our present situation. The hermeneutical questions, the questions of meaning and value, as well as the questions of decision and action, are presented to us in terms of our present. We ask the hermeneutical questions because we seek a way ahead in our situation that is consistent with who we are, as defined by our appropriation of the grounding Christian story of our existence. We also seek a way ahead that is responsive to the actions of God upon us. Thus we do not go to the narrative tradition empty-handed. We go with our questions and our needs in our present situation. If we faithfully retrieve the images and themes of the tradition, we are reminded afresh of who we are in the light of those images and themes. But we must do our retrieving search with appropriate suspicion—suspicion of ourselves and the distortions of our interests, and suspicion of the tradition's interpretations of the grounding story of the people of God. Thus each time we go to the narrative tradition, seeking a fresh understanding of who we are and who we are called to be, the tradition is put at risk, tested against our experience as we are tested against it.

Our hermeneutical inquiry is not, however, confined simply to retrieval from the tradition. It also involves our effort to respond to and appropriate in our actions the redemptive activity of God in the present as God, by the power of the Spirit, acts on our behalf to draw us and all created life toward the realization of

God's promise in the kingdom.[8] It is in response to this redemptive activity of God that our search for interpretations of our present situation that can open a way ahead for us finds those openings of possibility that would not otherwise be available. Here our perception of the possibilities of divine transformation of our situation is tested against the realism of what, given our situation and who we are in it, is possible. Here our memories of God's actions in the past remind us never to rule out the element of surprise.

Thus the center of the diagram attempts to show that through our hermeneutical inquiry in both directions, toward past and future, we are enabled to see our present situation through new lenses. We are enabled not only to see more clearly the normative imperatives that the Christian story presents to us, not only

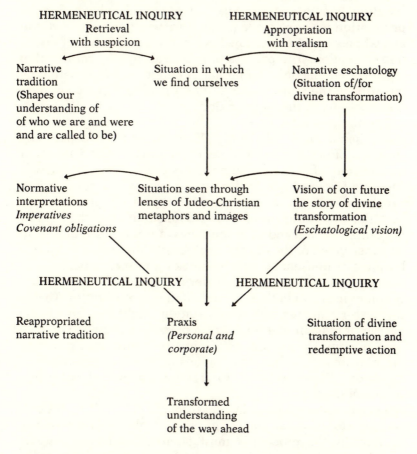

Figure 3. Narrative hermeneutics, human praxis, and the praxis of God.

our covenant obligations that direct our actions, but also a fresh vision of our future as made possible by the redemptive action of God. In the schema this is termed an "eschatological vision" to indicate that it is grounded in both hope and present reality, the reality of the "not yet."

The lower section of the diagram is intended to suggest that our human praxis, personal and corporate, is both an outcome of our hermeneutical reflective inquiry and a new situation calling for continued practical theological inquiry, decision, and action. The purpose of Christian praxis is to enable us to move ahead in our individual and corporate lives under the guidance of the Christian story of who we are, who we are called to be, and what the God of that story is bringing about. Thus in a sense the intention of the schema is that from the outcome at the bottom of the diagram we return to a new situation like that at the top, but now with whatever reappropriation we have made of the Christian narrative tradition and whatever vision we now have of the possibilities of divine transformation. The process of practical theological thinking is a never-ending one. Our human situation is an ever-unfolding one. It is in the midst of this story set in time that we discover the unfolding of the story of God.

Two things should be emphasized before moving on to test this schema on a case study. First, while I have used the situation of pastoral ministry as the content of the analysis of the tension of differing standpoints from which to view a situation (Figure 2), a similar set of tensions and perspectives can be visualized in the responsibility of all persons who consider the pluralism of their responsibilities in the light of the Christian faith and tradition. Thus, a similar diagram could be constructed of the multiple responsibilities of the head of a business or household, an educator or a farmer, a parent or a young person. To live in the modern world is to be in a tension of sometimes conflicting interests and responsibilities. That is the case no matter what one's station might be, though the degree of tension will differ from person to person. The widened horizon for pastoral care ministry involves the pastor in the ministry of guidance to persons amid the complexities of day-to-day life in relation to this multiplicity of roles and responsibilities.

Second, although the schema assumes a relatively intentional and therefore formal process of practical theological thinking, in actuality the process is most often much less structured. Practical theological thinking goes on in all kinds of ways and in various contexts. In a sense it occurs whenever and wherever persons ask questions about who they are and what they are doing. But a structured schema highlights just what is involved, whether the process is deliberate and reflective or more spontaneously unreflective.

4

Testing the Structure:
The Case of Centerton

With the formal structure of a narrative hermeneutical approach to the task of practical theological thinking before us, it is now time to test the schema on a specific situation confronting a Christian community and its pastor in a relatively typical American community. This example was presented by the local pastor in a seminar of which I was the leader. The report is slightly altered in order to protect the identity of the community and its citizens, but the persons involved, the community, and its situation are real and contemporary.

Context of the Situation

Centerton is a community of approximately 13,000 people in a somewhat mountainous area of a southeastern state. In years past the economy of the area was dependent upon coal, but for several years the mining industry in the area has not been doing well, and therefore the local economy has been on the decline. The town is, however, close enough to mountain resort areas to benefit from tourism.

As southern mountain towns go, Centerton has in its history been fairly progressive. It is an old town, founded around 1750 by the English, who hoped it would become a major city in the area. The early leaders of the community anticipated the possibility that the population might someday rise to 300,000 and the city become a center of both industry and trade. Accordingly, the town was laid out with wide streets and a spacious atmosphere. A golf club was developed early enough to boast of being one of the oldest in the United States. That club is still a center of Centerton's social life. The town does not boast a college, but there is one in a neighboring community. A new shopping mall has recently been constructed, which has attracted shoppers from a fairly wide area. There is an independent city school system and a community hospital. The minority population (black) is quite small, under 5 percent.

Religiously speaking, the town is largely Protestant and dominated by a high percentage of Baptist churches, though virtually all mainline Protestant denominations are represented. The ministerial association is not supported by the Baptists but is a thriving association which sponsors community services during Lent and Advent, as well as an annual Thanksgiving service.

The church of which I am the pastor is a congregation of 223 members in one of the mainline non-Baptist denominations. Traditionally it has the reputation for being the "country club church" of the town. The membership is largely well educated and in the middle-to-upper income level. Members are mainly professional people and persons who work in service and retail jobs. The turnover in membership is in recent years quite steady and greater than one might expect. The annual church budget for the coming year is approximately $80,000. Relatively speaking, as compared with other churches in the area, the worship is somewhat formal and liturgical. The church runs a nursery school in its facility and employs, in addition to the minister, three part-time people: a secretary, a janitor, and choir director/organist.

Recent history

The church. The church has for several years had a very poor image of itself. Until a year ago the church had seen most of its younger people leave to go to school or seek employment in other towns. There has been no new growth, leaving the church in a bind financially and in terms of volunteer workers. Indeed, the church desperately needs more and younger members with families in order to be able to offer the type of educational opportunities that would keep the church viable. Financially, the church has been supported by three principal families, who give over $6,000 each to the annual budget. The majority of other contributions are from persons at or near retirement and living on fixed incomes. Consequently, the church has been running behind in paying bills and denominational obligations.

The past year, however, has seen the addition of five new

families and the reactivation of several others, giving the church some sense of hope and new life. Attendance and contributions are also on the upswing.

The city. The city government has been a center of political controversy for many years. The city is currently under litigation from the national Environmental Protection Agency for failure to adequately treat waste, resulting in the pollution of the nearby stream, Brown Creek. The pollution was first brought to the attention of the city by Brown Creek Concerned Citizens (BCCC) some four years ago. This citizens' group brought suit a year ago for the same reasons that resulted in EPA's action. Charges of political corruption and mishandling of funds intended for the improvement of the existing sewage treatment facility led to the formation of another political action group, Citizens for a Better Centerton (CBC). They adopted a political agenda to oust the existing city council, who, in an effort to raise money for a new plant, raised sewer rates to an all-time painful high. At the most recent election CBC succeeded in electing a slate of people so that they now control the city council.

CBC has now set its sights on the mayor. Meanwhile, the city contends that part of the reason they are liable for the pollution is a local shoe and leather products manufacturing plant that does not pretreat its waste and often overloads the system. The manufacturing plant admits to a certain culpability but is also the city's largest employer. Its 450 employees add to the local economy and create much-needed tax revenues for the city. The plant is very run down, and the absentee owners are in a position to leave if the situation dictates.

Most recently, the newly elected council has rejected any notions of conciliatory behavior and in their first meeting fired all the mayor's political appointees, including the city financial secretary, police chief, and city attorney. There is much confusion as to the legality of these actions on all sides.

Other factors. Subsequent to completion of the new shopping mall, the Community Development Office was closed down by the city. The previous community development executive has a niece married to one of the church's strong financial supporters. He was fired by the mayor three years ago. The most recent community development director is currently attending the church. He was a political appointee of the mayor to the CD office after resigning as editor of the city's daily newspaper. Owing to accusations of "improper reporting," the state has chosen to close down this political office, and this has left Mr. D unemployed.

Other families in the church have often been on the wrong side of the political fence from the mayor. This has not gone unnoticed, nor has it been forgotten. Mr. B, the son of a former mayor, has recently left the church to go back to the First Baptist Church, which his parents attended all their lives. Mr. B's father was the only man successfully to oppose the mayor for office some four years ago. Otherwise Mayor C has held his office for twenty years with only that one interruption for a single term.

Cast of characters (the persons most directly involved)

Mr. A. Mr. A is thirty-four years old. His family owns the shoe factory and he manages it. He is from Detroit, where his father and his father's partner still live and operate the plant through absentee ownership. Mr. and Mrs. A have recently been attending the church and are developing a personal friendship with me as their pastor and my family. They have three children and are a devoted Christian family with a strong church stewardship background.

Mr. B. Mr. B is the son of Centerton's only other mayor in the past twenty years. His wife is still active in the church, though the two children now attend the Baptist church with their father. Mr. B is thirty-six years old and very outspoken. He is employed by his father in a hardware business.

Mr. C. Mr. C is the mayor of the town. A longtime member of the church and a strong financial supporter, he attends church about twenty times a year. Mr. C has recently had some respiratory illness and an automobile accident that required hospitalization. As his pastor I gave him considerable pastoral attention during that time. Recently he has developed a habit of calling his pastor late at night and taking me on "rides around town to talk." He is sixty years old. He has talked at length about the many allegations about his integrity and honesty in the use of his political office. I am privy to several confessions that bear out the truth of these allegations.

Mrs. C. Mr. and Mrs. C adopted one daughter early in their marriage. The daughter's son by her first marriage lives with Mr. and Mrs. C and his behavior has been a problem, particularly for Mrs. C. She has talked often with me as her pastor about these problems and now is in the habit of making daily calls either to me or my wife with news, gossip, and opinions about church affairs.

Mr. D. Mr. D is the most recent Community Development Director. He is now unemployed and having difficulty finding new employment. He is a loyal member of the church.

Rev. E, the pastor. I am thirty years old and have been pastor of the church for three years. This is the second church I have served, the first being a small congregation in a rural farming community. This is my first confrontation with power and wealth from a pastoral perspective.

Recent developments in the situation

Although the situation regarding environmental pollution continues to receive some media attention, the community at present seems apathetic concerning it. Recently there was a confrontation involving the ministerial association. That group decided to hear both sides of the issue (the mayor and BCCC) at two of its regular meetings. The mayor was hospitalized shortly before his scheduled appearance for medical reasons. During a pastoral visit to the hospital, I opened the subject of the mayor's appearance before the ministerial association. The mayor replied that he "felt that it was none of the churches' business what happened at city hall." He then went on to say that "he could never support a church that interfered with his work." Feeling this to be a veiled threat, I dismissed the issue, saying that I felt the mayor was being too defensive. I assured Mr. C that the intentions of the ministerial association were only educational. The topic has never been raised again. The pastoral relationship remains intact.

After giving the foregoing report of the situation in his church, the pastor then added two brief sections to his report to indicate his questions concerning his ministry in the situation. Those sections read as follows:

As pastor I have at least three arenas of responsibility:

1. A *kingly* function of administration to see to it that the church continues to run smoothly and well. That necessitates keeping an eye on our financial picture. The withdrawal of the financial support of the mayor could be a deadly blow to a church already struggling with finances.

2. A *pastoral* function to care for all the flock. I feel responsible to be able to remain in a position that allows me to minister to God's people in times of crisis and illness and to enable their spiritual growth.

3. A *prophetic* function to bear witness to the gospel. This entails for me some duty to speak out against sin and corrup-

tion and abuse of power, especially as it affects the poor and the oppressed who may not be able to speak for themselves. The abuse of God's creation is also a stewardship issue that may demand a prophetic voice.

In that light, these questions arise for me:

1. Where (and what) is the witness of the local body of Christ in this situation? It has remained disturbingly silent.

2. How does the pastor deal with an issue of known sin by an "upstanding" member of the church? To be sure, it is a case of abuse and corruption that is taken for granted by all concerned.

3. In the face of open intimidation, how does the pastor continue to carry on his pastoral functions to all concerned?

4. To what extent will the status quo and establishment be maintained for the sake of financial pressures and continued growth? Is there a means-and-ends issue involved here?

This concrete example of a situation of ministry illustrates my comment in chapter 3 that practical theological thinking must be done in the midst of an unfolding situation. We who read the report must begin thinking about it somewhere in the middle of an ongoing process. Even more existentially true is this for the pastor in whose place we must now try to locate ourselves. To use a simple analogy, practical theological thinking is like starting to watch a television movie in the middle. We have to pick up the thread of the story being unfolded before us without knowing exactly what went on before we tuned in. Practical theological thinking does not have the luxury of being able to begin at the beginning of the formation of the situation at hand. Nor can we analyze the forces at work in the situation in a detached manner, as from some ahistorical, transcendent position; to do that is to withdraw from the locus of the task. Practical theology begins within the limits of a concrete time and place and must move out from there.

The report also illustrates my earlier emphasis on the multiple action perspectives that make up the Christian community's life and work. When we think about the actions in the life and work of Christians involved in this case study, we must think about not only what they do together within the gathered community of the church, but also what they do separately and in various groups outside and beyond the church. Christian praxis permeates every arena of life where people called Christians are involved. In this case it includes the actions of Christians in the politics of city government, in the management of a factory, and in the activities of a concerned citizens' group and a ministerial association in ways that seem on the surface more significant than the activities that go on within the church building. The horizons of the range of activity that practical theological thinking must consider are indeed wide!

The Community and the Church

With these two considerations in mind, the need for beginning in the middle and the need for many action perspectives, the first question, "What is going on here?" becomes exceedingly complex. Yet this natural first question is undoubtedly the right first question. We need to understand first of all what is actually happening and what it may mean both to us and to the people involved. Then we can go on to ask what most crucially needs to be transformed. Our structure for practical theological thinking suggests that we do this by means of a narrative hermeneutical reflective process.

Using that approach, we are immediately aware that a number of interacting narratives with differing structures of meaning are at work in this situation. Those stories are interconnected in diverse and complex ways, but each story can perhaps be "located" in relation to a particular person or nexus of activity.

The "location" with perhaps the widest circumference of activity that is yet immediate to the situation is the town itself. Its story is one of considerable promise and expectation followed by significant disappointment. The town began with an identity filled with ambition. The wide streets are a daily reminder of the ambitious expectation that someday the town would be a thriving metropolis of 300,000 souls! But it was not to be. The mining industry on which the town's economy was built has dwindled and largely disappeared, and the largest remaining industry has been allowed to fall into disrepair. Not only that, but the remaining factory has been found to be polluting the town's mountains and streams, abiding objects of its pride.

What I am doing here, is attempting to put together, albeit in a very sketchy fashion, the elements of a plot or synopsis of a story of the town and its people as citizens of the town. In this way I have begun a hermeneutical inquiry into the present situation in the town by means of a reflective narrative as proposed in Figure 1. "What is going on here?" becomes "How did we get here and what out of our past tells us who we are here?"

Another important theme is the town's relationship to outside authorities. The pastor's report includes references to several "powers" outside who act or may act to change the direction of the story. The factory is owned by absentee owners who may arbitrarily close the factory. The tourists may come in greater or fewer numbers. The state fires the development director. One can surmise that the mining industry was shut down by decisions of outsiders. Now the EPA, truly a power from outside, has brought suit against the town.

The result of all these movements, among other things, is that, according to the pastor's report, most of the people are apathetic. A few are angry at the town fathers, who are blamed—rightly, if we are to believe the pastor's reports of nocturnal confessions—for the town's situation. One of the things that cries out for transformation, then, is the mood of the town. How can it be transformed from apathy into hope, from anger into joy in a sense of meaningful accomplishment? If pastoral care is given a horizon wide enough to include the atmosphere of a town, one of its purposes may well be that of transformation at this level. Care for the town becomes care for its emotional climate, its atmosphere.

If we follow the feedback loops of Figure 1, our brief dip into the story of the town's past now turns toward the future as the story being lived out projects or envisions it. That future "plot" may or may not be openly shared or acknowledged by the people of the town. If we were, like the pastor, actually in the situation, we would be listening for articulations or indications of that shared vision. Given simply the description we have before us, it would seem likely that the future of the story contains in some way projections of the past. The town waits for actions from outside to change the direction of the story—a new road through the area that would bring more tourists, a new industry that would offer new jobs and improve the economy. Meanwhile the people wait and grow more apathetic.

Imaginative reflection on this tentative story line quickly begins to collect around it a number of connections to some of the other aspects of the case study. The apathy of the church concerning its financial obligations, for example, may be seen as simply part of the larger apathy that pervades the situation. The tone of dissension that colors the pastor's report begins to make a more specific kind of sense than simply the human penchant for conflict. We know that apathy breeds discontent and discontent breeds dissension and blame placing. Apathy also makes possible the kind of power grabbing and corruption that has marked the town's recent history. It also can support the continuation in power of corrupt officials over the years when, as the report indicates, everyone has known and taken for granted that the corruption exists.

What I have been attempting to identify in the preceding paragraphs are not, in the empirical sense of the term, "causes" of the present situation. To look for causes would require a different kind of approach, involving scientific investigation of a wide range of factors. Such an approach would undoubtedly be useful in that it would perhaps uncover factors involved in the situation not apparent to us from what we now know about it.[1] The problem with scientific research in relation to the kind of practical theological thinking we are considering here is that it requires considerable time and expertise. Practical theological thinking done in the midst of a difficult situation of ministry usually cannot afford the luxury of either of those requirements. Pastors should be as "scientific" as is possible within the givens of the situation in which they are involved, but there is another level of thinking that can take place "in the midst" of whatever situation of human action is taking place. Seeing and interpreting the situation at hand within a plausible narrative structure makes possible envisioning a way ahead or appropriate response to the situation that opens the way for transformation.[2]

With the narrative theme of apathetic waiting and dissension at the level of the town's story in mind, we turn to the story of the church community. What does an attempt at reconstruction of that story reveal? We note first that the church has a history of being seen as the "country club church" in the town. That label connotes both pride in position and a certain sense of leadership in the community. It thus is important to the church to have the town's mayor and other leaders among its members. The fact that the mayor has been a major contributor has, of course, added to the importance of his presence. The formality of worship contributes to the portrait we begin to see of a church that values and must protect its tradition of prestige. Other factors have undoubtedly contributed to that as well, the generally higher level of education than the town average, for example.

But the church also counts among its members some of the mayor's chief opponents. The son of the man who once defeated him in an election was a member before he returned to the church of his parents. It would be interesting to know more about that decision, especially since his wife stayed behind. What did that mean to the people of the church? References to the eruption of dissension among the political opponents within the church context are notably absent. Why is that? Does the story of the church include an unspoken agreement that differences must be suppressed in that context? Does the need to maintain an appearance of the "country club church" prevent the admission of controversy there? Recall what I said earlier about the impact of pluralism in American life. Do we have here an example of fragmentation—the splitting of life into spheres or compartments that do not connect with each other? The absence of open dissension in the church may suggest an appropriation of the Christian story colored by a prohibition against the open airing of conflict. Does the fragmentation solution to the problem of pluralism link up with a form of Christian pietistic interpretation that suppresses conflictual differences? This opens some interesting possibilities before us with regard to the question of pastoral care of this congregation as a people of God. Does pastoral care of this congregation perhaps include introducing them to the possibility of confronting differences more openly, but in a context of a covenant of acceptance of one another as fellow members of the people of God?

If we follow the schema of Figure 1 in relation to the congregation and its story, our movement toward the future that congregational story envisions seems at first difficult. Reading the report, one does not get any immediate picture of the future toward which the congregation as a Christian community has directed its activity. The pastor does point to the addition of several new families to the church rolls in the past year. But he also points to a general situation of transient membership around a core of people who have been in the church a long time. One senses his hope for "new life" in the church, but the desire and expectation of the congregation in that direction is much less clear. One cannot help wondering if part of the price the congregation may be paying for retaining the appearance of lack of controversy in the church is not a dwindling of liveliness and genuine hope for the future. Again the possibility of pastoral care directed toward stirring the still waters that hide the differences in the hope of thereby stirring life into the anticipated story of the congregation comes to mind. One begins to think imaginatively about ways in which those waters might be stirred, various scenarios of liveliness that might be possible.

The schema of Figure 1 suggests a parallel process to that of the present-past-future-present narrative reflection on the situation in both town and congregation; namely, a similar reflection on the primary Judeo-Christian narrative. As in the case of reflection on the stories behind the situation at hand, this reflection may take multiform patterns, both in private reflection and congregational or small-group inquiry.[3] Our search here is for narrative themes, images, and metaphors that may further illuminate our hermeneutical reflection on the stories of congregation and larger community. The reflective process may be careful and systematic, such as planning a series of sermons to contribute to the pastoral effort toward transformation. It may be an educational process, such as an adult church school series of discussions. Or it may simply involve the pastor's or layperson's own private effort to gain perspective on the situation at hand.

As we move toward the Christian story in its past tense we take with us the themes of apathy, anger, dissension, fragmentation, and unacknowledged corruption, along with the need for new hope and transformation. As in the case of our earlier reflection, these themes begin quickly to collect biblical metaphors, images, and stories about them. Dissension reminds us of situations of dissension in the biblical narratives—the tower of Babel, the dissensions among the disciples, a number of stories of the Old Testament, the prophets speaking about the controversies of the time and the corruption of human purposes. The liveliness of these texts strikes us afresh as we bring them into friction with the themes we have carried with us from the situation at hand.

> And the LORD came down to see the city and the tower, which the sons of men had built. And the LORD said, "Behold, they are one people, and they have all one language; and this is only the beginning of what they will do; and nothing that they propose to do will now be impossible for them. Come, let us go down, and there confuse their language, that they may not understand one another's speech." (Genesis 11:5–7)

> For from the least to the greatest of them,
>   every one is greedy for unjust gain;
> and from prophet to priest,
>   every one deals falsely.
> They have healed the wound of my people lightly,
>   saying, "Peace, peace,"
>   when there is no peace.
>   (Jeremiah 6:13–14)

> And when the ten heard it, they began to be indignant at James and John. And Jesus called them to him and said to them, "You know that those who are supposed to rule over the Gentiles lord it over them, and their great men exercise authority over them. But it shall not be so among you." (Mark 10:41–43)

Here what might be called the pluralism of the Bible—that is to say, the rich variety and variability of its stories and perspectives—becomes both a helpful resource to our imaginative hermeneutical retrieval of images and themes that connect with the situation at hand and a problem for careful hermeneutical work in interpretation of the familiar texts. The schema therefore includes a degree of suspicion. The biblical materials must be allowed to speak to us and, in a sense, make their own connection to our situation. A hermeneutical conversation among our perceived themes in the situation, our prejudices (the term is used in a nonpejorative sense) concerning both situation and biblical text, and what the text has to say to us must take place. The schema portrays this as a process of mutually critical correlation, the outcome of which may be a fusion of the horizon of the biblical text and its metaphors and themes with the horizon we bring from our reflection on the situation in which we find ourselves, so that our understanding of both text and situation is opened to new possibilities.

The situation in the Centerton church and its community suggests not only the texts just quoted but a wide range of texts that have been passed down to us from the early Israelite community. I am lured into dialogue with those texts by their portrayal of both apathy and dissension, both of a community struggling to declare its identity under God and of a community perpetually straying into corruption and loss of the vision of who they were called to be. That dialogical memory leads me to recall the narratives of the prophets and their dramatic efforts to recall the people of Isreal to the covenant narrative that had shaped their identity since Abraham and the Mosaic covenant of Sinai. Most profoundly, I am led to recall the stories of the faithfulness of God in all human circumstances, in all the twists and turns of the biblical narrative.

> A voice on the bare heights is heard,
>   the weeping and pleading of Israel's sons,
> because they have perverted their way,
>   they have forgotten the LORD their God.
> "Return, O faithless sons,
>   I will heal your faithlessness."
> "Behold, we come to thee;
>   for thou art the LORD our God.
> Truly the hills are a delusion,
>   the orgies on the mountains.
> Truly in the LORD our God
>   is the salvation of Israel."
>   (Jeremiah 3:21–23)

Space does not permit here the full detailing of the possible connections that may be made between the biblical narrative and the narrative tentatively proposed for the situation in the

Centerton church and its town. The schema allows for a rich and virtually inexhaustible possibility of retrieval. The schema also proposes that, whatever the level of biblical hermeneutical reflection that may be undertaken, a turn toward the future that the biblical narrative envisions should be made so that there may be mutually critical correlation of that vision of the future with the vision embodied in the situation of the church and town. That correlation will begin to rub together those expectations and the images of hope and promise of God's transformation through the power of the Spirit, images of resurrection and the continuing activity of the living Christ in all places where there is apathy and dissension, failed hopes and corrupt promises.

Here, of course, the schema of Figure 3 becomes important as a structure for our narrative hermeneutical inquiry. That schema invites us to hold open before us the possibility that the transformative activity of God may already be present in the situation at hand in ways that we do not identify or are not able to anticipate. Reflecting on that captivating notion, I cannot elude the tantalizing possibility that somehow in the confluence of forces and events, relationships, and people that make up the confused and fragmented situation of Centerton, God is already bringing into being a new and transformed reality. The processes at work in that situation may, as they play themselves out, usher in a new community that breaks through the reality of the old one. If that be the case, then pastoral care for the people of God may not be so much a process of forcing the changes we might like as of shepherding God's people through a time of transition and change in ways that open them to respond to the transformative activity of God at all levels of their lives.[4] That practical theology of expectation needs, however, constantly to be held in tension with a practical theology that informs human actions. The people of God are called upon both to wait for the salvation of God and to govern their actions by the normative requirements of the Christian narrative tradition.

> From of old no one has heard
>   or perceived by the ear,
> no eye has seen a God besides thee,
>   who works for those who wait for him.
> Thou meetest him that joyfully works righteousness,
>   those that remember thee in thy ways.
>   (Isaiah 64:4–5)

The Mayor

Our testing of the narrative hermeneutical structure for practical theological thinking in relation to the Centerton case has focused on the two communal levels, that of the town itself and of the Centerton church. We need now to test the structure by relating it to more individual concerns, for practical theological thinking goes on at many levels. We shall first consider the situation of Mr. C, the mayor of Centerton, and then we shall turn to the pastor and his situation.

Even though a superficial reading of the case study seems to suggest Mr. C as the villain of the piece the schema we are using asks that we first look at the situation through his eyes. What is he experiencing, and what does that experience mean to him? Careful pastoral use of our schema, because it assumes that any situation will take on a different meaning depending upon from whose perspective it is seen, demands that individual perspective be given respect and an open hearing. Here, of course, we wish that the pastor had been more generous with the details of his conversations with the mayor.

Seen from Mr. C's perspective, the situation must be at this juncture a very difficult one indeed. Not only is he faced with the legal actions of the EPA against him and his administration of the town's business, but the strength of his opposition in the town has recently increased substantially. No longer does he have a friendly city council to support his actions. His appointees have been dismissed by his political enemies, who now hold the upper hand. Furthermore, he is caught by the situation in regard to the shoe factory. The owners' irresponsibility with regard to pretreatment of their sewage has brought on the crisis in regard to the environment and thus opened up to public scrutiny some of the mayor's past actions that helped create the problem. Yet he cannot press the operators of the factory to help solve the problem because the disaster of the loss of the factory to the town must be avoided at all costs. Mr. C is in a tight spot. Meanwhile, at home he must cope with a gossipy spouse and a grandson to raise who is himself creating problems. While it is perhaps too risky to surmise that Mr. C, at some level of consciousness, is vaguely aware that his grandson's misbehavior may be related to his own past actions, one cannot help wondering if Mr. C does not feel in some way responsible. Thus we can imagine that in both situations, his work and his home life, he may be feeling responsible and yet impotent to act to alleviate his misery. His recent illnesses and his automobile accident are evidence of the level of pressure he is under, occurrences in which he is at once the responsible party and the victim.

Mr. C has turned to his pastor for support, though we are struck with the peculiarly ambivalent way in which that reaching out for help has taken place. The pastor has already communicated his availability during Mr. C's hospitalizations. So, like Nicodemus, Mr. C now seeks out his pastor in the dark of night. He cannot ask directly for help; that violates his long-standing image of himself as the man of power and leadership. One wonders if, by driving around the town with his pastor, Mr. C does not in some symbolic sense preserve that image of being the leader of the town. One also senses that Mr. C must in some way connect his troubled situation with a vaguely conceived religious or moral frame of reference. He does talk about his past reprehensible actions. But from the report it would appear that the disclosures lack the ring of a sincere confession. The relationship with the pastor must retain a note of intimidation. Like many persons of power, Mr. C finds the price of humble admission of guilt and helplessness too high to pay openly. One wonders if the climate of the faith community, a climate we have already seen to be one that suppresses conflict and pain, has not participated in making it more difficult for Mr. C to seek the guidance and forgiveness he needs from his pastor. The past story of outward respectability and prestige that covers hidden fault and corruption must be maintained.

Here we should note the necessity of intermixing several languages and modes of interpretation in the process of practical theological reflection on a situation such as that of Mr. C. We can see from a psychological perspective, that Mr. C is suffering from intense situational anxiety as a result of events that have thrown him into an acute identity crisis. His ego, probably falsely inflated over many years by virtue of his position, is greatly threatened. Both as the powerful mayor of the town and as partner in a marriage that supports his image of being the one in charge, his narcissistic self-image has sustained itself. Now on both those fronts he is suffering from considerable narcissistic injury. In that situation his self-doubt, so long suppressed, reasserts itself. Dynamically speaking, that conflict between inflated narcissism and self-doubt has, it would seem, been somatized in his illnesses. Thus the inflated self-image is preserved while yet the self-denigration and guilt are expressed.

At another level, however, the language of individual psychology is not fully adequate to account for and interpret what is going on with Mr. C. His psychological difficulties are taking place within a larger social matrix that is also dynamically at work. The languages of social psychology and sociology also offer useful perspectives with which to consider the question of what is going on. The mayor is in many ways fulfilling a role thrust upon him by the community. This fulfillment has facilitated and thereby in part made possible the continuation of the atmosphere of apathy within the town. Social psychologists such as Richard Sennett would say that Mr. C has fulfilled for the town a paternalistic role that has deep sociological roots in the development of such social roles as that of "boss" in the evolution of capitalist society in America.[5] The predicament he is in is therefore not one entirely of his own making, which, of course, should not be taken to mean that Mr. C may be morally excused from his responsibility in the situation.

This last comment serves to remind us that the situation of Mr. C needs to be understood from the perspective of moral reflection and its language of analysis as well. Clearly Mr. C may be said to have acted and perhaps continues to act in a morally irresponsible manner. By his own admission he has violated the trust placed in him as an elected official. We can surmise that he has used the powers of his office for his own rather than the citizens' benefit. The injustice and inequity of his acts need to be recognized and a confrontation take place relative to his responsibility to act in ways that, insofar as possible, restore the situation to conformity with what is lawful and morally just. Theologically speaking, Mr. C may be seen as now being subject to the judgment of God as that judgment is mysteriously hidden in the events that are confronting him with the fruits of his past actions. Pastoral care of Mr. C cannot escape the obligation to help him both to acknowledge his responsibility for past acts and to act responsibly in the future.[6] The practical pastoral problem is one of methodology. How can Mr. C best be offered the opportunity to come to terms with his moral responsibility in ways that, given his limitations as a person, he can accept without retreating into the shelter of his inflated narcissism?[7]

If we follow the schema of Figure 1 in our hermeneutical reflection on Mr. C's situation, we will not only use a wide range of disciplinary perspectives to gain understanding as to how Mr. C's situation developed to its present state, we will also be able to project that situation into the future it implicitly contains. Here Mr. C's story becomes indeed clouded. We can anticipate that his political enemies will continue to harass him and, if possible, drive him out of office in disgrace. We can also antici-

pate that his inability to resolve the environmental problems of
the town will end in a costly legal defeat at the hands of the EPA.
Thus his narrative myth of power is destined almost inevitably to
end in tragic disappointment and perhaps fatally injured pride.
We begin to envision the necessity of helping Mr. C come to
terms with the illusory nature of his grandiose self-image. How
can the pastor utilize the intimacy of his nocturnal visits with Mr.
C to open up the question of Mr. C's future?

Here our reflection on the biblical story may prove illuminating. If, for example, we select any of the Old Testament prophets
as a focus of our retrieval of biblical themes and images, we are
confronted with stories of great courage and risk taking on the
part of the prophets, but also stories of prophetic utterance that
consistently remained faithful to a commitment to the welfare
and future destiny of the people of God. The prophets often spoke
strong words of confrontation. But those strong words were
contained within a relationship that passionately communicated
care and concern for the people to whom the words were spoken.

Thus Jeremiah, in unmistakable language of rebuke, cries:

> Thus says the Lord:
> "What wrong did your fathers find in me
>   that they went far from me,
> and went after worthlessness, and became worthless?"
> (Jeremiah 2:5)

Or again:

> "For my people are foolish,
>   they know me not;
> they are stupid children,
>   they have no understanding.
> They are skilled at doing evil,
>   but how to do good they know not."
> (Jeremiah 4:22)

And yet:

> Thus says the Lord:
> "The people who survived the sword
>   found grace in the wilderness. . . .
> I have loved you with an everlasting love;
>   therefore I have continued my faithfulness to you."
> (Jeremiah 31:2–3)

Abraham J. Heschel, the Jewish biblical philosopher and theologian, in his monumental work on the prophets of Israel, says of the style and force of prophetic approach:

> Authentic utterance derives from a moment of identification of a person and a word; its significance depends upon the urgency and magnitude of its theme. The prophet's theme is, first of all, the very life of a whole people, and his identification lasts for more than a moment. He is one not only with what he says; he is involved with his people in what his words foreshadow. This is the secret of the prophet's style: his life and soul are at stake in what he says and in what is going to happen to what he says. It is an involvement that echoes on. What is more, both theme and identification are seen in three dimensions. Not only the prophet and the people, but God Himself is involved in what the words convey. [8]

This commentary suggests that the possibility for fruitful confrontation of Mr. C's moral responsibility by his pastor will be enhanced to the degree that the pastor is fully identified with Mr. C in his situation *and* to the degree that both he and Mr. C can experience the stake and involvement of God in the outcome of both their conversations and of the larger situation in which they find themselves. If we place ourselves in the position of the pastor, these reflections raise sharply the question as to our level of involvement with Mr. C and the entire situation in Centerton. We cannot hope to be pastorally helpful if we seek to confront the situation from some outside position that does not share the stake the people involved have in it or the stake that God's care involves. Here our appropriation of the past, present, and future dimensions of the Christian narrative takes on crucial significance, since by the fusion of the horizon of our understanding of Mr. C's situation and our pastoral involvement in it with that larger narrative horizon we are reminded both of the importance of our full and empathic presence in the situation and of the limits of our responsibility. Final outcomes of the story of Mr. C and of Centerton are held within the outcome of the ultimate story of God. The realization of that undergirding control and support is a realization both of limit and of freedom to risk.

The Pastor

We have already begun to turn toward hermeneutical reflection on the situation from the perspective of Pastor E. The schema of Figure 2 opens the issues involved from that perspective still further. We have seen that the pluralism of action perspectives from which the parish pastor must both interpret any situation confronting the ministry of the church and act within that situation places the pastor always in a dialectical tension between or among action perspectives. It is evident that Rev. E recognizes that tension from the manner in which he raises his questions concerning the case. His listing of three levels of pastoral responsibility, the kingly, the pastoral, and the prophetic, indicates his sense of the overlapping and at points conflicting claims of those responsibilities. Figure 2 suggests that these conflicts, as Rev. E confronts them, are inherent in the role of pastor of a community of faith. They assert themselves critically in a time of crisis such as that in which Rev. E now finds himself, but in actuality they continually define the dialectical limits within which the role of pastor must be fulfilled. How is that multidimensional dialectical tension to be resolved in the case of Rev. E and the Centerton church?

The pitfall into which many pastors are drawn in response to this question is analogous to that described in chapter 1 in the discussion of fragmentation in the face of cultural pluralism. Many pastors find themselves tempted to be prophetic interpreters of the faith tradition in the pulpit in relation to social-situational problems, pastoral shepherds in their involvements with their parishioners in relation to their individual situations of sickness and health, marital problems, and the like, and business administrators in relation to the institutional maintenance of the church. That pastoral "solution" can lead to the fragmentation of meaning worlds, and pastoral identity loses its integrity and consistency of purpose. Pastor E's relationship with Mr. C confronts him with the opportunity and necessity of integrating the four action perspectives of Figure 2 in the concreteness of their conversations. The formulation of his questions in the report suggests that Rev. E is likewise confronted with this necessity as he prepares his sermons and leads the congregation in confronting its stewardship problem. To be sure, in many situations of ministry, one of the four action perspectives schematized in Figure 2 may be dominant and the others in a more recessive or background position, as Seward Hiltner's classic *Preface to Pastoral Theology* suggests, but in the dynamic movement of changing immediate contexts of ministry within which the day-to-day work of parish pastors takes place, constant attention must be given to the integration of action perspectives in both thought and pastoral act.[9]

Our earlier consideration of Mr. C's situation suggests that it is just such integration of pastoral action perspectives that is needed if the stalemate in the narrative direction of Mr. C's life is to be broken open to a more hopeful possibility. A careful reading of the manner in which Rev. E has presented the material of the case suggests that in a sense Rev. E is caught in a similar stalemate. He is acutely aware of the need to confront the moral and theological dimensions of Mr. C's situation. He also seems aware of the implications of his ministry to Mr. C for the future course of the church's life and that of the community at large. Yet he has found himself relating to Mr. C in ways that avoid the confrontation and offer false reassurance. His fear to act otherwise seems from his account to be directly related to his fear that the pastoral relationship with Mr. C will lose its "intact" quality. In the background one also senses his fear concerning the possible loss of Mr. C's contribution to the church budget. What is he to do that will balance all these considerations and yet open a transformed future for both Mr. C and himself, along with a possibly more open future for the church and community?

The Activity of God

It is at this point that the schema of Figure 3 becomes crucially significant for our narrative hermeneutical inquiry. Figure 3 seeks to put before us both the transformative possibility inherent in incorporating the lenses of Christian metaphors and images into a way of seeing any situation in which we find ourselves *and* the realistic appropriation of a vision of the possibilities of transformation of our situation through the redemptive and transformative activity of God. What would it mean for both Rev. E and Mr. C if the power and meaning set forth in Figure 3 could be appropriated in their relationship and praxis in the situation with which both are confronted? At this point we can, to be sure, only speculate about that. But it does seem clear that if Pastor E can to some significant degree incorporate into his pastoral presence with Mr. C an awareness that he is not alone in his desire and determination for transformation, the climate or atmosphere of the situation will be drastically altered. The presence of God in the situation is, at one and the same time, a judging presence that confronts Mr. C with the unfaithfulness of his actions, a faithful presence that is willing to suffer risk with Rev. C, and a mysteriously powerful caring presence. With that realization, a certain hopeful confidence in the ultimate outcome will become more dynamically operative, as well as a certain acceptance of the present involvement of God in even the harsher and more painful aspects of the situation as it is taking place. Such an awareness may free Pastor E from enough of his fear of self-risk as well as

the impasse he is experiencing concerning the conflict of pastoral responsibilities that he can at once mediate the care of God
to Mr. C and open up the moral responsibility issues with him. It
may indeed be possible for Rev. E to see that the pastoral lever
that has been placed in his hands by Mr. C's ambivalent request
for pastoral care is just the lever that, by the grace of God, may
pry open the apathetic, stalemated situation of the Centerton
church and community.[10]

When I speak of the transformative caring presence of God in
the situation of Mr. C and his pastor, I am speaking of a reality
only to be appropriated in faith. From our human perspective we
are involved in an ambiguity and a mystery. The transformative
presence of God is not a power that we can direct or appropriate
for our own purposes. The pastoral temptation when in situations such as here described may well be to attempt to use an
awareness of God's presence as a club or lever in a power move
with Mr. C: to say, in effect, "You must face up to this moral
problem because God and I together say you must!" To fall into
that temptation would be to fall into the same power tactics so
characteristic of Mr. C in his past dealings with people. Rather,
the pastor in this situation does well to seek to communicate to
Mr. C that both persons are subject to the judgment, the merciful
care, and the transformative power of God. The Spirit of God is
active with them in their mutual effort to work through the
situation in which they find themselves in ways that are ulti-
mately redemptive for all concerned.

Much more could be done with these narrative hermeneutical
reflections on the case of the Centerton church and its people.
There are other key figures in the situation: Mr. A, for example,
whose role in the Centerton problem merits analysis. He is in a
peculiarly difficult position as the representative of the absentee
owners of the factory and as one who is in process of finding a
place for himself in a new community. His growing friendly
relationship with the pastor presents both pastoral opportunity
and possible conflicts of interest. Our mode of practical theological thinking is one that is continuously in process. The passage
of time and new events require continual reworking of interpretations of events at hand. New decisions must continually be
made, new actions undertaken in response to perceived changes
in the situation. Likewise new insights into both the situation and
the Christian narrative tradition through whose lenses one
attempts to see the situation in theological perspective create

new situations of praxis that must be recycled through the hermeneutical inquiry process.

There are likewise implications in the Centerton case that are pertinent to consideration of the interlocking dynamics of what are often considered as separate "functions" or "practices" of ministry. I have in mind here the interplay of preaching, administration, church and community ministry, and the like. The narrative hermeneutical approach to practical theology within which the foregoing analysis of the Centerton case has been undertaken proposes a mode of reflection that has the potential for bringing these various functions of parish ministry into a much greater degree of coherence than is often the case in typical pastoral practice. It is beyond the scope of this book to consider in detail the implications of narrative approaches to practical theology for pastoral functions other than pastoral care. However, it is important that the implications of such approaches at least be acknowledged.

My purpose here has been to test the structure for a narrative hermeneutical approach to practical theological thinking. Insofar as the Centerton case is concerned, this approach has brought into focus a number of important elements at work in the Centerton situation that shape pastoral practice options. Other approaches may yield perspectives and possibilities that this approach fails to emphasize. However, the approach detailed in this chapter offers rich and varied possibilities for directly relating traditional Christian metaphors and narrative themes to other ways of interpreting human problems at many levels. Thus the task of practical theological thinking is enriched and the process of interpretation kept lively and open.

5

The Pastoral Task:
Guiding the Interpretive Process

In this chapter our attention will turn toward the specific role of the pastor as symbolic leader and guide of the Christian community in the context of modern life. I want to explore some of the dimensions and ambiguities inherent in the pastoral role and to propose as a "center of gravity" for that role the image of the pastor as guide of the interpretive process of the people of God.

The Role and Authority of the Pastor

The role of the pastor in the congregation has in a number of ways become problematic in the modern context. Here may be seen yet another impact of pluralism. In that context even the faithful have come to assume that modern life requires many specialized authorities. Although the pastor may still be recognized by many as the community's authority in regard to such matters as biblical interpretation and talk about God and God's activity, pluralism has greatly eroded for modern congregations any notion that the pastor has commanding authority or knowledge about many things of concern to them in everyday life. Likewise, recent developments within the churches themselves have moved toward vesting more and more of the authority of the church in the lay congregation, with less dependence on direction from the ordained clergy.

These shifts in perception of pastoral authority may be visualized clearly by reflecting on the problematic status of the three metaphorical images from which Rev. E, the pastor in the Centerton case study, was attempting to draw his understanding of his role conflicts.

Rev. E lists those images as king, pastor, and prophet, although they are traditionally given the designations prophet, priest, and king. Rev. E, however, is correct in his wording to the extent that in its pastoral care usage in recent times the term *pastoral* has been metaphorically skewed in the direction of the priestly tradition and away from the more socially aware and ethically motivated prophetic tradition. In its avoidance of authoritarian behavioral direction it can also be seen as deemphasizing the "kingly" function of ministry. Be that as it may, all three images drawn from the Old Testament covenant tradition point toward a certain hierarchical authority. "King" denotes the political authority of command. "Priest" denotes the ecclesiastical authority of cultic power. "Prophet" denotes one who speaks with the authority of God. In the modern context, at least that of Western culture, most such hierarchical authorities have been in significant ways deauthoritized, and in their place have been installed the authorities of specialized knowledge. In that situation the pastor is left with only his or her specialized knowledge concerning such things as the Bible and theological traditions conceived in a relatively narrow fashion.

One result of this shift in pastoral authority is that in many matters of concern to Christians the atmosphere of decision and action has become much more democratic and egalitarian than was formerly the case, even in the so-called free churches. Pastors may seldom any longer speak as from some hierarchically defined position of authority. Rather, the pastor's right to be heard and taken seriously is defined more in terms of the parishioner's perception of both the reasonable wisdom (specialized knowledge) of what is said and the quality of relationship communicated. Thus, although the pastor's authority has been deemphasized, there are significant gains in that pastoral access to the everyday experiences and problems of genuine concern to the lay Christian has been opened up in ways more nearly devoid of some negative aspects of a hierarchically authoritative relationship. In that atmosphere a relationship of mutual exploration and reflective consideration of options may be possible. The loss of hierarchical authority may in that case facilitate greater freedom in the relationship for both parishioner and pastor.

These shifts in pastoral authority make the image of the pastor as guide perhaps somewhat as problematic as those of king, priest, and prophet, though possibly in less hierarchical terms. Insofar as the word *guidance* connotes paternalistic or authoritarian right to command obedience, it too becomes problematic in the more democratic atmosphere that now prevails within the churches. In the modern context the authority of command has largely shifted to the workplace, where a hierarchy of ownership and management prevails and the "boss" may exercise commanding authority, but only within the contractual limits of employment. Participation in the life and work of the church has in modern terms been strongly colored with the connotations of voluntarism and individual choice.

The image of pastoral guidance has, however, a long history generally recognized as having its formative roots in the New Testament. [1] In Jesus' response to the questions and concerns of individuals, as well as in the accounts of the early formation of the church in Acts and the epistles, may be found the earliest Christian narrative accounts of pastoral guidance that gave shape to this central aspect of the role of ordained leadership in the Christian church. Along with healing, reconciling, and sustaining, the image of the pastoral role of guidance has functioned as a controlling image for the work of the pastor in relation to the care of souls.[2] The specific significance and methodologies of guidance have been subject to alteration over the centuries as they have been influenced by important changes in the social milieu, but the image as an organizing metaphor for pastoral care of persons has remained central to the role of designated pastoral leadership. Since the early nineteenth century, the mode of pastoral guidance has become increasingly eductive in response to the social atmosphere of privatism and individualism in relation to religion and participation in the church.[3]

The guidance image seems to be worth preservation in an age in which persons are searching for sources of practical wisdom concerning ordinary problems of living that combine commitment to a structure of religious meaning and faith with knowledge of the complexities of modern life. It denotes a style of attending to the welfare of God's people in the modern pluralistic context that combines both leadership and nurturing care, both a certain pastoral wisdom in matters of importance for living and yet the recognition that the people of God are much of the time scattered in widely differing arenas of life about which the pastor has only limited knowledge. The modern context requires, therefore, that hierarchical authority be softened considerably.

I want to further qualify the image of guidance by associating it with the use of the term *interpreter* or *interpretive*. This qualification places a limit on the authority of the pastor in relation to command or direction and suggests that the most appropriate exercise of pastoral initiative in the modern context is at the point of interpretation of both the Christian narrative tradition and the contemporary living situations being confronted. In the modern context the pastor does not have the right or authority to command or direct. Whatever vestiges of that authority that may remain are rapidly disappearing, and good riddance! But the authority to clarify, to interpret, to guide understanding remains, and upon that authority the pastor may build pastoral guidance relationships with persons in all manner of modern situations.

We have seen that to be identified as a member of a Christian community is to embody the intention to have one's identity shaped by a certain narrative, the Christian narrative of the world. But to live in the modern world is necessarily to have one's life and identity molded and shaped by various other stories of the affairs of the world. For the Christian this creates the problem—which is at the same time an opportunity—of sustaining one's identification with the Christian story while going about the ordinary tasks of life in the modern world, life that may be shaped by another story or confluence of stories. Thus to live a Christian life today necessarily involves making sense of the events and relationships of life within a profusion of narratives, a complex variety of stories of what life is, what it is about, and what it should be. To live life as a Christian therefore inevitably involves a process of interpretation and the resolution of tensions among various interpretations of the many activities that make up modern life. That is the case whether or not a person self-consciously seeks to be an interpreter of life. Even the most unself-conscious making sense of one's relationships or the events of one's life involves interpretation: interpretation that makes use of the metaphors and images, the themes and symbols of the pluralism of stories within which one's life is being lived out.

It is precisely because we live among a plethora of varying interpretations that even the most sophisticated of Christians will often be in need of an interpretive guide. The hermeneutical process required by modern life becomes complicated and confusing. Stories of what is right and true about life cut across each other in ways that bring conflicting interpretations. The vision of the Christian life becomes clouded by the subtle presence of other narrative visions of the good and the true. A wise and caring conversational partner is needed in the search for truth or the best way ahead. It is in that role that I wish to cast the pastor as guide in relation to the interpretive process of God's people.

We began with the simple proposal that the word *pastoral* itself contains the central meanings that shape the task of pastoral

care. The word connotes a particular source or origin for the
care that is given, its origin within the community, and its tradition, which the pastor represents. The word also connotes a
certain respect and attention to the particularity of the human
situation toward which the care is directed. We saw that the task
of pastoral care is located in the tension between these two
concerns, the one linked to the community and its grounding
narrative, the other linked to the particularity of the human
situation at hand and its location in modern life.

Thus there is a certain parallel between the situation of the
ordinary Christian who must sustain his or her Christian identity
in a pluralistic context by a process of interpretation, reinterpretation, and action in the varied contexts of everyday life, on the
one hand, and the situation of the pastor who must sustain her
or his role as representative of the Christian community and its
narrative while attending to the particularity of the human situations that are encountered in the varied contexts of day-to-day
ministry. Both involve interpretation and actions based upon
interpretation. Both involve the recognition of the tensions
between various modes of interpretation rooted in differing stories of what the affairs of the world are about. There is also a
parallel in that both parishioner and pastor are in a situation in
which the interpretive process must issue in some form of intentional action.

Viewed from the standpoint of this parallelism, a central purpose of pastoral care ministry comes more clearly into view.
Pastoral care should be directly related to the facilitation of the
various "ministries" of the laity in the world. It finds its fulfillment in the enablement of Christians to be the people of God in
the world. Pastoral care is not simply related to the personal and
private lives of parishioners, as much of recent pastoral care
practice would seem to indicate, given its emphasis on personal,
psychological, and relational problems. Rather, pastoral care
involves the pastor's care-filled relationships with members of
the Christian community in ways that facilitate bringing their
various activities in the world into closer and more meaningful
coherence with their commitment to the Christian story.

The thesis of this chapter emerges out of this recognition of
the parallelism between the ministry of the lay Christian and that
of the ordained pastor. This thesis proposes that the "center of
gravity," so to speak, for pastoral care ministry can best be found
in acknowledging that the purpose of pastoral ministry and the
purpose of Christian life are both to be fulfilled in the shared
praxis of life. That shared praxis takes place both in the commu-

nal context of the church and in the scattered individual contexts of the daily lives of Christians. As a gathered community the church develops modes of shared praxis through its worship, educational, and mission activities. Scattered in widely varying individual locations in the world, Christians share the task of relating all these worldly activities to the meanings found in the Christian story. In either case the task involves making use of the narrative structure of Christian faith as a primary framework for the overarching interpretation of the activities of life in all its pluralism of contexts and purposes.

Seen in this light, the task of pastoral care is found in the facilitation of the interpretive process of the people of God in ways that enable the members of the Christian community to find that unity for living which is the dominant need of persons in modern life and which, according to the Christian narrative understanding of the world, Christian interpretation alone can adequately provide. In the language used in chapter 3, following David Tracy, this means that the task of all Christians and the parallel task of pastoral work among lay Christians by ordained pastors both involve the mutually critical correlation of all the various languages and stories that inform the multiplicity of actions in which Christians are involved.

Inherent in this formulation of a "center of gravity" for both Christian life and pastoral care in the modern context is the assumption that no one metaphor or controlling image is adequate to encompass all the ramifications and considerations that must be taken into account in the complexity of the modern situation. Rather it is necessary that a rich pluralism of metaphors inform both Christian praxis generally and ministry praxis in imaginative ways so that the interpretive process is kept open and lively.

The case of the Centerton church and community illustrates the importance of richly pluralistic metaphorical interpretations. Rev. E, the pastor who prepared the Centerton case study, sought clarity about his various role relationships (what he termed "arenas of responsibility") as pastor of the Centerton church by use of three metaphors: that of king, pastor, and prophet. His brief explanation of those metaphors articulated the role conflicts he was experiencing as a pastor sensitive both to the dimensions of his calling as a Christian minister and to the pressures of his situation. As I suggested, Pastor E's dilemma seems to have several dimensions which, taken together, threaten to leave him unable to act decisively. If he asserts the prophetic function to which he feels called, both his pastoral role as he understands it and his "kingly" responsibility as administrator of the institutional church are potentially threatened. On the other hand, if he acts with the primary intention of keeping the "pastoral" relationship, most particularly that with Mr. C, intact, his prophetic role in relation to Mr. C and the larger community issues are both undercut.

As Rev. E formulates the dilemma, and as he reports his actions in the case, it would appear that his interpretation of his kingly responsibility controls his response to the situation in ways that undercut his sense of prophetic calling and undermine his sense of pastoral integrity in relation to Mr. C, whom Pastor E sees as a person who needs to confront his wrongdoing and find forgiveness issuing in a new direction for his life. The center of gravity of Rev. E's ministry appears to be his kingly role as administrator of the institutional church. That particular function has taken charge of his action decisions in his ministry. To be sure, from his expression of anxiety about keeping the pastoral relationship with Mr. C intact, it may be inferred that what he terms his pastoral responsibility competes with the administrative for his primary loyalty. But neither of those two functions seems to provide the unifying image for his ministry that he seeks.

Thus the Centerton case illustrates the difficulties encountered when any single organizing metaphor for ministry, even when grounded deeply in Christian narrative sources, becomes the dominant or controlling metaphor. In that situation the shape and direction of ministry becomes distorted, its purpose skewed by a particular metaphorical perspective that threatens to become idolatrous and blind to the broader spectrum of ministry possibilities. It is in the careful and imaginative tending of the interpretive process itself that unity of ministry purpose and action can best be found. Such tending involves making use of the rich pluralism of metaphors for ministry that are available from the narrative tradition as well as those metaphors that come from other ways of seeing the world now available in the modern context.

Pastor E's effort to understand the impasse of his ministry by use of the king-pastor-prophet set of metaphors does, however, open a further consideration in the use of traditional metaphors in ministry. While it is in certain ways clarifying to say that the task of parish pastoral ministry embodies the three defining metaphorical images of king, pastor, and prophet, simply to assert those metaphorical images fails adequately to come to grips with the diversity and conflict inherent in those images. It may be, however, that a more careful retrieval of the full narrative context from which these images emerged will serve to bring those images into greater coherence and prioritizing order. Here the structure of narrative practical theological thinking set forth in chapter 3 may demonstrate its applicability.

The prophet-priest (pastor),-king metaphors for ministry have their origin in the Old Testament narratives of Israelite history and were shaped in significant ways by the historical process of the people of Israel beginning with the period of the patriarchs. In the earliest historical period of Israelite history the monarch was a chieftain thought to be endowed with divine powers who exercised all three functions: priestly, prophetic, and royal. In the course of time these functions became separated and distributed among different individuals. The king took control of military power, and, while he kept a presence as religious leader, retaining the aura of divine power, the actual priestly functions were taken over by others.[4] So there developed through the movement of Israelite history a considerable tension among the several strands of covenant tradition, each identified respectively with the cultic priests, the kings who were heirs of patriarchal authority, and the prophets—those who emerged from time to time as both critics and passionate spokespersons for the will and judgment of Yahweh. Thus there are deep roots in the narrative tradition that speak of the necessity of keeping those three imagistic sources of religious authority in some degree of tension and balance. The stories of Israel's history tell of periods during which either the cultic authority of the priests or the worldly power of the kings became overbalanced and the covenantal vision of the Israelite people as the people of God was in danger of being lost. It was at those times that the prophets moved to call the people back to the primary loyalty to Yahweh and the central purposes of covenant life.[5]

Reflection on this narrative history of the prophet-priest-king set of metaphors sheds considerable light on Rev. E's conflict of priorities concerning his ministry. While such reflection acknowledges the importance of both the administrative (kingly) responsibility for the institutional life of the congregation and the priestly concern for Mr. C's loneliness and isolation, it gives central priority to actions and relationships that preserve and further the covenant meanings for the total life of the people in relation to God and God's purposes. Interpretation of both situation and organizing center of purpose for ministry is enhanced by keeping that meaning-grounded fulcrum of understanding in

its proper central place. Insisting on that is the central thrust of
the prophetic ministry tradition.

> Neither prediction nor speaking in the name of God is the most
> important feature of biblical prophecy. The prophet is not sent to
> the people in order to demand that some particular act be done; he
> is sent because of a divine concern for the total existence of the
> people; he does not convey primarily a command *ad hoc*, but a
> message that relates to the total existence of the people.[6]

Here Abraham Heschel asserts the principal implication of the
prophetic tradition for the task of pastoral care ministry. To be
true to that tradition, the pastor does not view the pastoral task
as that of making demands for particular ways of acting in the
world on the part of Christians acting singly or as a community.
Rather, the pastoral task is to see that the concern of God for the
total existence of God's people is acknowledged and taken into
account. To be sure, when that concern of God is accurately
represented, the priority of certain ways of seeing and interpreting situations and of certain actions over others may become
apparent to all concerned. But, as the schema of Figure 3 suggests, the fulcrum of the pastoral task has to do with sensitivity
to the actions and purposes of God in all human historical
situations.

This brief historical analysis of the prophet-priest-king metaphors leads to the tentative conclusion that Rev. E's formulation
of his dilemma as a conflict among his three levels of responsibility may itself in a crucial sense be faulty. The center of his
concern from which all his interpretations and actions need to
emanate should, according to the narrative tradition from which
those images come, be one of sensitivity and response to the
concern of God for all arenas of human life and activity. Neither
pastoral nor kingly, nor even, at least in the narrow sense of
advocacy, prophetic responsibility can carry the weight of being
the organizing center of Pastor E's ministry. Rather it is repre-
sentation of the concern of God for all of life and the interpretation of all situations of life from within the meanings that emerge
from that controlling concern which alone provides the fulcrum
on which Pastor E's ministry can be balanced.

At this point the modern pastoral care tradition needs to be
both affirmed and evaluated critically. In the mid-twentieth century, much pastoral care became focused on situations of extreme
personal and relational stress: personal crises of living such as
sickness and death, bereavement and loss, marriage and family
crisis, and the like. From a theological standpoint its central
focus was the concern of God for persons in extremity, even

though this focus has been at times obscured by the growing dominance of psychological interpretations. However, by focusing pastoral attention primarily on the private, individual, and interpersonal relational life, other arenas were left largely unattended or seen as the concern of forms of ministry other than pastoral care. In that situation pastoral ministry threatens to become, like so much of modern life, fragmented and lacking in coherence of purpose. One result may be that pastors like Rev. E will tend to experience their pastoral care of persons like Mr. C largely in a privatistic framework. Only when the mutually critical interpretive process itself, with its central concern for the activity of God and human response to God's activity in all of human existence, is restored as the center of gravity for pastoral work with the people of God will the diverse contextual pressures of ministry regain coherence of purpose. The horizons of what pastoral care is or can be will be greatly widened beyond the privatized arenas of personal relationships, and the central fulcrum of pastoral concern will be both clarified and made more unitary.

The Pastor as Guide of the Interpretive Process

With the notion of pastoral guidance of the interpretive process in place as the central fulcrum for pastoral care ministry, I wish now to turn our attention toward filling in some of the details of the day-to-day implications of that conceptualization for what the minister does in the ordinary work of pastoral care. To what will the pastor attend? Where will the pastor attempt to locate? What will be the qualities that mark the pastoral relationship as one of interpretive guidance? Can a rough-hewn phenomenology of such a role, together with a suggestive list of its locations, be developed, not as a "cookbook" or detailed technical guide for hermeneutical pastoral care but as a portrait or model of the role? Keep in mind that our interpretive guidance model for pastoral ministry has important implications for virtually every aspect of the minister's work in the congregational context.

Communicating to the reader what I have in my mind as the portrait of the interpretive pastoral guide is like painting a portrait. The broad outlines can be sketched in quickly. The pastor is a listener and interpretive guide. The pastor's goal is to help persons find meanings in what goes on in their lives that stitch those events and relationships into the central meanings of the Christian story. The pastor listens for the potential conflicts and

congruencies between other stories informing the activities of
life and the Christian story. The pastor attends to that interpretive
task both in such public roles of ministry as the weekly Sunday
sermon and in day-to-day relationships with the people. This
outline can be made in bold strokes like those of a line drawing.
But details must now be filled in to give the portrait greater
specificity. What does this portrait of the role mean in *this* specific human situation? In *that* one which seems very different
from the first? As we attend to the details, the broad outlines
become at once less clear and more necessary. The problem of
maintaining clarity of outline with specificity of detail develops
into a tension. I cannot say that this and not that is what the
pastor does in every case. Yet the pastor-as-interpretive-guide
outline necessarily asserts itself as the controlling image. How to
fill in the details and retain the sharp clarity of the outline is the
problem.

There is an analogy here between my problem in writing and
the problem of the pastor in the concrete situation of ministry.
Desiring to retain clarity of outline in the guidance role, the
pastor too must deal with the multiplicity of details of the differing situations at hand. The outline of the pastoral task that the
pastor has in mind does not always exactly fit the scope and range
of the details of the situation that demands the pastor's response.
Attending to those details in all their specificity and uniqueness
can quickly blur the outline of the task. A tension develops here
also.

The analogy may be pressed still further by relating it to the
primary analogy around which this chapter is constructed, that
between the interpretive life of Christians generally and the
interpretive task of pastoral care. To be a Christian in the modern
world is something like painting a portrait. Christian meanings
provide the outline, but the details of the portrait must be filled
in, using the materials at hand in whatever modern context the
Christian may be located. Attending to those details while keeping the basic outline clearly in focus becomes an artistic as well
as an analytic task that on some occasions can be complex and
difficult. It is at such times that the presence of an artistic interpretive pastoral guide can prove most helpful.

In essence pastoral care practice in this interpretive guidance
mode is more than anything else an effort in metaphorical,
analogical thinking that results in softly focused verbal gestures,
actions, and relationships which will vary significantly in differing situations while yet retaining a central interpretive purpose.
Such pastoral work requires a deft and lightly imaginative touch,

a ready eye for connections and analogies, and the ability to make use of images and themes that come to life in the situation at hand. At the same time, it also requires that the pastor cultivate the capacity to keep a steady eye on the central goal of Christian praxis: the grounding of all of the stories of life in the Christian story of God and the world. It cannot be done successfully with a heavy hand and a stubbornly determined effort to put Christian theological labels on every set of human circumstances or daily events. Carried out in that fashion, pastoral care will soon become exaggeratedly formal, even lugubrious, and lack sensitivity to the nuances of particular situations. Thus its method is more like writing poetry than it is like scientific analysis or the formal explication of Christian dogma. It is an art, not a technique or an academic exercise.

Interpretive Pastoral Care Issues

Let us now turn to a phenomenological effort to fill in some of the details of the portrait of pastoral care in the narrative hermeneutical mode. The scene to be examined is the ordinary day-to-day one of pastoral work as the pastor moves from place to place and time to time in the course of her or his daily rounds. That scene includes the usual variety of administrative duties, parish meetings, hospital and home visits, street corner and telephone conversations, community activities in which both pastor and laity are involved, longer conversations in the pastor's study initiated by either pastor or parishioner, and times of individual, family, or community crisis. All these times of pastoral presence provide occasions for interpretive pastoral care.

In uncovering the phenomenological content of such pastoral contacts, the notion of the presence of meaning issues is central. In other words, in virtually every significant pastoral contact there will be present, latently hidden or manifestly apparent, issues that have meaning and significance for living, many of which will have direct or indirect implications for living the Christian life. The pastor's presence, whatever the occasion, has particular metaphorical or symbolic significance because of the pastor's role as interpretive guide. The quality of this significance will vary from occasion to occasion and may be quite different for the pastor than for one or another parishioner. Phenomenological inquiry thus offers potentially fruitful possibilities for fleshing out the portrait or model of what the task of pastoral guidance is.

We shall now consider the issues with which pastoral guidance primarily concerns itself. What issues will the pastor be listening for, the presence of which, in whatever pastoral situation, will signal the opportunity for interpretive pastoral care?

Issues of personhood and life cycle

In the modern period, we have become accustomed to thinking of pastoral care as fundamentally and primarily a ministry to persons as they seek to cope with life. The good pastoral guide seeks therefore to know people personally. That means not only seeking to know each person in some sense intimately and individually but always having one ear tuned to the significance of whatever happens to the individual. The pastor will also be attuned to the particular significance of whatever happens in the outside world as it affects that individual. The pastor is thus not simply concerned with the significance of events as they affect the general welfare of the community or the world; the pastor is concerned with the impact of events on the personhood of persons.

Here, of course, the mutually critical correlation of psychological and theological ways of thinking and speaking about personhood and the significance of events for personhood is very important. Listening for the issues of personhood means in part listening to hear what is happening to persons psychologically. How are they coping with the stresses and strains of living? Are old personal psychological issues getting in the way of their full experience of life: issues of self-acceptance and self-denigration, self-confidence and insecurity, narcissism and dependency on others for approval? The more we learn from the psychological perspective concerning the human life cycle, the more we are aware that many of the issues of personhood emerge from the changing tasks and dilemmas of the cycle of life from birth to death.

But the pastoral guide listens for these issues of personhood and life cycle with an ear attuned to these issues as they may be framed finally not so much in the language and narrative framework of psychological ways of interpreting them as in terms of how those issues may find a frame of reference—an ultimate resting place—within the Christian understanding of the meaning of individual life. Thus the pastoral guide listens for opportunities to consider with the person what it means to be an individual living within the limits of a historical life cycle while yet being held within the mystery of what it means to be an individual child of God. The pastoral guide seeks to help the individual intimately and personally to an awareness of that mystery, and, of the security it can provide for living out one's personhood with integrity and faith. On occasion, when the time is right, the pastor may speak directly of that mystery. But on all occasions of relationship to persons, the pastor will seek to represent the good news of that mystery and the placing of the issues of personhood in its frame of meaning.

In my book *The Living Human Document*, I speak of these issues of personhood as the deep issues in the life of the soul.[7] That formulation assumes that issues of the soul take form within a nexus of forces and meanings that bring together the particularities of individual human psychological development, the equally particular contextual social situation that surrounds the person, and the ways of interpreting faith and value that make up the cultural milieu in which the person is embedded. Issues of the soul present themselves in multifarious ways and wear many different disguises, and they are seldom presented to the pastor directly in religious language. The pastor is therefore always having to translate the language of their presentation into language recognizably religious or theological. Much of that translation will take place in the pastor's own mind as the stories of individual and life-cycle conflict are heard, often in fragmentary form. The question as to how and when the translation into Christian language should be shared is a difficult and delicate one, which calls upon the artistic and communicative capacities of the pastor.

A brief account of a relatively routine pastoral contact reported by a pastor will illustrate how issues of personhood and life cycle are often presented:

Phyllis Jasper, an attractive thirty-nine-year-old housewife, dropped by the pastor's study while out running errands for her busy businessman husband. The conversation was casual and easy at first, focused on what appeared to be simply the sharing of recent events in an active life filled with the tasks of home and husband.

After a time the conversation seemed to run down. A short silence was broken when Phyllis said rather abruptly, "My head is full of thoughts about all the things I have said I want to accomplish with my life, but my body these days seems to be telling me to slow down. I'm having a problem keeping my head and my body together. Do you suppose I could be going through a mid-life crisis? Maybe my body is telling me to relax and accept the inevitable."

The pastor, aware from previous conversations with Phyllis of her long-standing disappointment over the inability to have a child, responded simply, "Sometimes bodies do seem to have a mind of their own."

There followed a thirty-minute serious conversation between pastor and parishioner that touched on a number of related topics without apparent resolution of any of them. Phyllis reported on the latest effort she and her husband had made to pursue adoption. She also reported on her last visit to her physician, a specialist in problems of infertility. Nothing physical seemed to be wrong, but, even with the expensive medications and tests, her last menstrual period had occurred right on schedule. "What is wrong with me, do you suppose? Why did God make it so that some women who do not want children can have them so easily while I who want one so badly cannot? My time is getting short, and Bill is several years older than I am."

"It's frustrating and disappointing not to be able to get your body to do what you want it to do, isn't it? I wonder what your body is telling you about life? Bodies do seem to have a greater wisdom than heads sometimes."

"Well, my body sure seems to be saying to relax and let go of something. But it is so disappointing and I feel so incomplete!"

"Do you suppose God could be disappointed along with you? Maybe he too is often frustrated by the incompleteness of things. There are a lot of things in creation that seem incomplete."

The conversation continued along this line for a few more minutes. It ended when Phyllis seemed ready to stop. The pastor knew that they would talk again when the time seemed right to Phyllis. He felt no need to wrap things up with a little homily or a formal theological statement. Phyllis left to return to her errands, and the pastor returned to his study.

Whatever may be our critical judgment about the pastoral care offered Phyllis Jasper, it is useful to think of this conversation as an effort at interpretive pastoral guidance. Phyllis is trying very hard to make sense out of her disappointment and frustration in not being able to control her body. In the conversation may be heard echoes of a number of different narrative accounts of that problem. Phyllis readily appropriates the current popular understanding of the life cycle and wonders if she is experiencing a mid-life crisis. We also hear echoes of an old philosophical story of mind-body dualism. The American story of success and accomplishment hovers in the background, as does the ancient human story of blame and the taint of guilt. But Phyllis is also trying to stitch her experience into the Christian story of God and God's participation in the affairs of humans in the world. She searches for a resolution and resting place for her disappointment in that story of religious meaning. And in his gentle, somewhat fumbling way, the pastor seeks to help her. The effort involves what I have called mutually critical correlation of perspectives. It involves allowing theological reflection to be loose and spontaneous enough to make both intellectual and emotional contact with Phyllis and her struggles. More than anything else, it involves patience and the willingness to enter into a common praxis with persons experiencing life as it is, grounding that mutual praxis in the identifying narrative of Christian faith.

Issues of relational responsibility and interpersonal conflict

Issues of personhood rarely, if ever, take place in a relationship vacuum. Rather, the issues of the soul tend universally to involve those relationships with persons that are of primary significance to the person. For most adults this means the relationships with spouse and family. For some single adults, the lack of such relationships within a nuclear family of one's own becomes a focal issue, while for others the arena of these issues simply shifts to that of intimate friends and extended family. For young people it virtually always means relationships with parents and peers. It also frequently means relationships with work supervisors, neighbors, and vocational peers and colleagues. Not infrequently these relationships cut across each other and generate loyalty conflicts, conflicting obligations, and tensions of conflicting interests. They also almost universally generate conflicts between personal concerns and needs, on the one hand, and felt responsibility for the needs and expectations of significant others. Questions as to whether and how in the flow of busy and pluralistic life "my needs" are to be met or "my desires" are to be fulfilled make up a great deal of the content of self-concern in the modern context.

The pastor is very often directly or indirectly sought out as a friendly and authoritative listener to stories of these relational conflicts. In a peculiar way the pastor symbolizes to many people both the concern of God for the fulfillment of individual needs and the obligation of persons to be relationally responsible. That double symbolism itself sometimes creates a peculiarly significant dynamic ambivalence in the parishioner-pastor relationship. The pastor is thus now and again thrust into a simultaneously advantageous and painfully difficult position as guiding arbitrator of need-responsibility conflicts.

Pastors in this position can err on either side of the need-responsibility equation. Sensing the other person's need for affirmation, the pastor may too quickly reassure the person of his or her right to have personal needs met. Such reassurance certainly has ample grounds of legitimation in the biblical and Christian theological tradition. But so likewise does the legitimation of the primacy of responsibility for the needs of others. It is essential, therefore, that the pastor keep clearly in mind that the great commandment at the center of the Christian narrative tradition holds these two concerns in tension: "Thou shalt love thy neighbor as thyself."

In the fragmented context of modern life, however, this conflict is given a peculiar shape and direction, not infrequently experienced by persons as an impossibly difficult double bind. Fragmentation as a cultural condition can evoke a powerful sense of legitimation for the primacy of self-interest as the only viable alternative to being pulled in too many obligational directions at once. This "solution" to the relational problem creates narcissists, persons who see all of relational life as an arena in which to get their own needs, and desires fulfilled, come what may.

For other persons, no less self-oriented, the only viable alternative may be seen as life lived as a constant effort to satisfy every obligation. Not infrequently, this relational stance harbors an equally self-oriented expectation that, in return, others will be obligated to fulfill one's own needs. In neither case has the need-responsibility equation been properly balanced. Indeed, the central meaning of responsibility contained in the commandment— namely, the command to so care for the needs of the self that the self is able to *respond* to the needs of others—is lost.

It is perhaps useful to consider this relational problem of modern life as revealing a kind of continuum with relation to the self-other orientation. If I am correct in my psychological observation that overweening concern for obligations harbors a hidden self-interest, the continuum becomes a virtual circle, rather than a polar tension. Schematized, however, as a polarized tension, the continuum takes the form sketched in Figure 4.

This continuum reveals the manner in which a relational stance characterized by either pole subverts the meaning of responsibility, which requires a simultaneous consideration of both self and other needs. The pastor, as representative of the Christian narrative understanding of what human relationships were meant to be, will always take a stance in or near the center of the continuum, seeking to assist the person in the maintenance of a relational posture that holds total obligation and the effort at self-sufficient exploitation of others to fulfill one's own needs equally at bay.[8]

The sensitive pastor will be constantly involved in the mutually critical correlation of Christian narrative understandings of the meaning of responsibility and psychological and sociological perspectives on the structure of human relationships. Traditional Christian theological meanings of responsible relationship need to be critically correlated with other more scientific understandings of human relational dynamics in order that the Christian perspective may be enriched and critically reappropriated to fit the modern contextual situation. Likewise, the psychological and

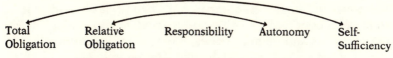

| Total | Relative | Responsibility | Autonomy | Self- |
| Obligation | Obligation | | | Sufficiency |

Figure 4. The self–other relational continuum.

sociological modes of analyzing and interpreting human relational problems need the constant check of confrontation and questioning by the interpretive standards of the Christian tradition. It is that narrative tradition that the pastor fundamentally represents; so it is primarily the insights of that tradition that will mark most significantly the pastoral stance in regard to human relationships.

Issues of choice and life-style

The impacts of pluralism on modern life have not by any means been all negative, despite the fragmentation pluralism has brought. Pluralism has, in ways that have sometimes been salutary, tended to loosen the tight social controls that particularly white middle-class standards of respectability have had until recently on American life. Conformity to middle-class patterns with regard to all manner of choices that affect the quality and shape of daily living had, by the mid-twentieth century, tended to become stultifying and stagnant. This domination of the culture by the white suburban middle-class life-style had tended to skew the struggle to achieve freedom and autonomy for many persons, young and old, in ways that were fundamentally harmful to the human spirit. Whether the struggle issued in automaton-like conformity or rebellious refusal of the authority of cultural standards, the results were often persons crippled in their capacities to exercise freedom creatively. Not only have middle-class standards often been based on the shallow values of appearance and materialism, these standards also have tended to isolate persons growing up in middle-class society from the suffering of the poor and from the oppression created by a culture of affluence. Young persons who by accident of birth grew up in family situations that did not conform to the standards of affluent respectability were made to feel left out of the cultural vision of the good life.

One of the impacts of pluralism has been to begin to break up this taken-for-granted dominance of the traditional white middle-class life-style. At virtually all levels of American life, with the exception of the lowest level of the culture of poverty, there is present to a significant degree a climate of freedom to choose one's way of life. Social controls have been relaxed with regard to the expression of sexuality and marital relationships, conformity to dress and manner codes, the desirability of one place of residence over another, and the like. The exercise of what is often referred to in popular culture as "preference" has been given a new social legitimation.

As is most often the case with cultural changes that represent societal efforts to "solve" what have become cultural problems, this swing of American culture toward greater libertarianism has brought its own problematic elements. Persons living in an atmosphere that places highest value on the exercise of freedom of choice can begin to feel at sea, with little to guide them, in the choices they must, by the cultural value standard, now make for themselves. At once the range of possible choices becomes diffuse and open-ended, while the pressure on the individual to "make the right choice" is greatly increased. Meanwhile, the continuation of demands for social conformity in significant areas of social life—such as, for example, the business world or the local church—makes for a cultural atmosphere of mixed messages with regard to one's right and responsibility to choose. With the coming of the 1980s, a new climate of conformity threatens again to take control in ways that confuse and combine conformity to the culture of affluence with an idolatrous valuing of self-indulgence.

The parish pastor who keeps eyes and ears open cannot help being bombarded with awareness of a great variety of situations in any parish where issues of choice and life-style are becoming acute. They arise in nearly every family that includes young people moving from adolescence into adulthood. They are present in countless households where women are choosing whether or not to work outside the home. They are frequently in evidence in marriages in which one or both partners have come to recognize the bland conformity of their public and private life-style. They are experienced by men who, after years in the same profession or job status, begin to feel stifled and restless and become aware of a longing for the freedom to change before it is too late. Housewives who have faithfully reared their children and now long for a chance to do something "on their own" agonize over the issue of how and where and why and "Who will have me with my rusty skills?"

For the pastor who can structure everyday pastoral work among God's people around the image of interpretive, reflective guidance, the presence of any of these issues of choice and life-style may be seen as occasions that call for interpretive reflection and conversation. The values and perspectives of the modern situation of open-ended choice and increased freedom need to be brought into dialogue with the values and perspectives in the Christian understanding of what life was meant to be and the possibilities and limits of human choice. This ministry sometimes may require a reinterpretation of the biblical texts that speak of obedience as conformity to the covenant will of God. It may require a reappropriation in fresh terms of the meaning of freedom and growth into "the stature of the fulness of Christ." Most of all, it will require sensitive listening to the stories of struggles to choose and conflicts of values accompanied by reflective questioning and musing together with persons as they search for new or reappropriated guidelines by which to govern their lives. In short, it will require pastoral guidance in an inquiring hermeneutical mode that meets persons where they are in the midst of their choices.

Issues of vocation and work in the world

An important sector of modern life within which questions of choice and life-style arise is that of participation in the work of the world. So predominant is the arena of work in determining the content of daily life that issues related to this arena deserve special consideration. In the modern world, persons are primarily identified by what they do for a living. Ask who someone is, and the typical response will refer first of all to the work that person does. Adult persons are bankers, lawyers, housewives, secretaries, laborers, migrant farm workers, or store clerks before being identified as anything else. In that social reality itself lie a host of issues with which the person must in some way come to grips or make peace in order to feel participant in the human community. Not only that, but every vocational identity, whether chosen or fallen into by default, carries with it a set of issues and problems that impinge on all other aspects of living as a human being in the world. That is true whether one has been fortunate enough to choose a professional identity, such as that of a physician or teacher, or has by circumstance, lack of opportunity, or level of ability been pushed into menial work like that of a laborer or garbage collector.

I have deliberately designated this set of issues those of vocation *and* work, since it is in the tension between the work actually to be done and the sense of vocation about that work that many of the issues arise. The words *work* and *vocation* are by no means synonymous. Work refers simply to the activity itself, the work that is to be done for which one is paid a given sum and granted a certain status by society simply because of the value placed upon that work by society. Therein, not incidentally, lies yet another nest of issues that have moved to the fore with the pluralization of modern life. Women are not paid as much as men for comparable work. Certain tasks are devalued by society, even though they are crucial to the welfare and future of the society. Professionals in sports are paid vast sums for playful work while teachers of the young, who must not only work long hours on the job but take work home with them that occupies their evenings, are poorly paid. Housewives, who most often work the longest hours of all, rarely receive any monetary remuneration and are said to "not work." Inequities and injustices with regard to work and its rewards are rampant in the workaday world.

The tension to which I refer with regard to work and vocation, however, includes not only these tension over inequities but the tension between the work to be done and the meaning of that work, its capacity to fulfill one's vocation, that even the most advantageous of occupations contains. Many of the issues for which the pastor will be keeping an ear tuned in the course of pastoral rounds are those related to struggles with one's sense of human vocation, one's calling in the world, and the work one does. Here again, the potentially most useful stance will be one of interpretive guide and conversation partner, who listens for opportunities to stimulate consideration of these issues from within the framework of meaning provided by the Christian gospel and its tradition.

Issues of corporate responsibility, social justice, peace, and the future of humankind

Here the circle of issues widens markedly from the boundaries of those issues that directly and immediately involve the individual. Much of the human activity that structures the quality of life is corporate activity, activity that involves small or large groups of individuals acting together. Whether the structure is political, as in the case of a unit of government; legal, as a so-called private corporate unit or company; public, such as a business corporation; or voluntary, like the association form of a church or community organization, groups of people take joint responsibility for carrying on an activity together. Such conglomerate units of persons make decisions, exercise power that affects the life situations not only of themselves but of others, and thereby form a socially constructed world. The larger the unit that has been formed, the less directly does the individual participant experience personal responsibility for the unit's actions. If, for example, "the company" decides to open a factory in Thailand or Honduras in order to exploit the country's cheap labor, the individual employee, whether a lower-level factory worker or an upper-level management executive, experiences the decision as somehow removed from individual responsibility. Even more is that the case when governments make decisions that affect the quality of life of millions of people the individual citizen will never know.

Here lie a host of issues that are present, if most of the time hidden, in any community. Much of the time parishioners may think briefly and more or less distantly about these issues as they read the daily newspaper or watch the television news programs. They may ponder them more deeply or even agonize over them when occasions arise or events occur that directly affect themselves or their neighbors. But most of the time these issues simply hover in the background unattended. They seem either too big or remote to be dealt with or too impossible of solution. The world of problems and issues for which one can take responsibility must be kept small enough to seem manageable. One can have an impact on the quality of life of one's family, though even that may seem unmanageable at times. One may exercise responsible power in the decisions of one's church or the PTA. If one owns a company, one can try to see to it that customers and employees are treated fairly and an honest product is produced. One can be a responsible citizen of one's neighborhood and even try to vote intelligently in the election of representatives to government. But beyond that what can one individual do to affect issues of social justice and the need for greater corporate involvement in the creation of a truly human world?

An incident in the work experience of a young ministerial candidate provides an example of how issues at this level can suddenly become compelling when heretofore they have been kept at a distance.

Don Brister came to seminary primarily to attain the requisite credentials for serving as a pastor of small rural churches in his home state. He had grown up in a small conservative church, felt comfortable there, and looked forward to returning to be pastor to "some good country folks." Theologically Don thought of himself as an evangelical Christian. The parameters of his ministry interests were largely confined to preaching biblically oriented sermons and relating warmly to the individuals in the congregations he was to serve.

Since Don needed to support himself while in school, he sought part-time employment and felt himself fortunate to meet the owner of a small metal fabricating company at the church he began attending upon arrival at seminary. The man gave Don his business card and suggested he call for an appointment. "We need someone to help out with keeping up with the payroll. We can probably use you." Don noted that the business card featured a slogan reading, "We operate a Christian business." That slogan, Don discovered upon going for his interview, was repeated on large signs posted here and there throughout the company plant. In his report of his experience, Don recalled that he "felt fortunate to be working in a Christian atmosphere."

Don found the job at first to be just what he needed. The work was not hard. It paid well, and his employer let him know that he should feel free to work on his seminary studies as much as he needed to while on the job. "You are preparing for the Lord's work and that should take priority."

Soon, however, Don began to make some disquieting observations. Working with the payroll, he became aware that many of the employees, some of them with years of experience working with the company, were paid at or near minimum wage. Furthermore, there were a few who, like himself, were paid a much better rate and given special privileges denied to most workers. He began to wonder about the meaning of the company slogan. Quite apparently, his employer was in most ways sincere in his Christian intentions, but beneath the surface there were inequities and unjust practices. Don began to suspect that the Christian slogan was covertly being used as an advertising device.

By the time Don reported his experience in the seminar I was teaching, he was beginning to reconsider his understanding of his ministry vocation. Issues of corporate justice, economic power, and class prejudice were beginning to become very real and urgent. At the center of this new consciousness burned the disquieting fire of his own privileged position. He asked his classmates to help him consider the issues he now wanted to confront and work with him concerning options he might consider. Should he quit the job, even though it was an easy way to work his way through school? Should he confront his employer and risk being tossed out? What about his long-term plans for his ministry? Did they need to be changed?

This young would-be pastor's consciousness-raising experience is almost a caricature of countless experiences that occur to ordinary Christian people again and again in the workplaces of American life. It is a caricature of the way in which for many the great societal issues of economic injustice, corporate exploitation, and class inequity become concrete and specific. Unfortunately, most often these experiences of confrontation with such problems are passed over, left unexamined, or rationalized in ways that avoid taking their implications seriously. They are, however, the experiences that, if shared with a sensitive interpretive guide or if reflected upon with fellow Christians under the guidance of an interpretive leader, can transform the consciousness of Christian people concerning their responsibility for their fellow humans.

Traditionally, pastors have not tended to think of these issues as being within their purview while going about the work of pastoral care. Being public issues, they have been thought of as better addressed in the public ministries of preaching and denominational or community organization. Pastoral care deals rather with matters that directly relate to individuals or families. If the truth were known, that limiting of pastoral concern probably is analogous to the limiting of the individual parishioner's list of issues to be concerned about to a world that seems manageable. To seek to address the large and nebulous issues of corporate responsibility, social justice, and peace as the pastor makes parish rounds seems too great an undertaking, too nebulous, impossibly difficult.

Yet these issues are increasingly, even overwhelmingly, urgent and in subtle ways are present in the day-to-day conversations and relationships that flow through the work of pastoral care. Pastors who listen will hear persons express their concern for these issues or, perhaps more frequently, hear echoes of the suffering that their parishioners are experiencing for themselves or for others, directly or indirectly brought about by human actions at this corporate level. Sometimes these indications of suffering simply need to be heard and set within the context of a framework of Christian theological meaning. This may be done not by delivering a theological treatise or applying a theological label but by the gentle usage of a familiar Christian metaphor or the asking of a theologically framed question. At other times the pastor's relational and symbolic pastoral "weight" needs to be thrown behind the mobilization of the individual's sense of corporate responsibility and capacity for generating corporate power and influence.

Whatever form the pastoral response may take to the hearing of the cry of the people for social justice and peace in the world, the fulcrum or center of gravity of the pastoral response will come from the interpretive effort to locate these issues in the abrasive yet hopeful proximity of the Christian narrative tradition. That tradition, particularly in its prophetic and eschatological strands, emphasizes the crucial importance—indeed, the controlling reality—of human communal and corporate decision and action. It declares human connectedness, embraces the welfare of even the stranger, and calls the total human community back to covenant relationship with the one who is Lord of all the world.

Pastoral care ministry can contribute to the effort to confront the great issues of justice and peace, the corporate care of the people of God for all the people of the earth, as pastors both invite and respond to direct and indirect invitations in homes and on the street corners to converse and reflect on these global issues. The fact that they are large and unwieldy, often nebulous and clouded by controversy and lack of clear solutions should not deter us. We need to remember that in the stories of our tradition, it is often the "still small voice" that speaks to change the world, the tattered remnant of the people who build the future.

Issues of truth and the ultimate meaningfulness of human existence

While the issues of justice and peace for which humans have corporate responsibility seem so large as to be unmanageable, the issues of ultimate truth seem imponderable, to the average person too deep and mysterious to be understood with any clarity. Echoing the sense of inadequacy of the author of Psalm 131, many ordinary folk in the Christian community have said in effect to themselves:

> O Lord, my heart is not lifted up,
>   my eyes are not raised too high;
> I do not occupy myself with things
>   too great and too marvelous for me.
> But I have calmed and quieted my soul,
>   like a child quieted at its mother's breast;
>   like a child that is quieted is my soul.
>
> O Israel, hope in the Lord
>   from this time forth and for evermore.

This short psalm of childlike trust is one of the loveliest examples of the use of feminine, mothering imagery in the Bible. It expresses the humility of humans before the mystery of the imponderable, ineffable mystery of human life in the care of God. It likewise reveals the deepest anxieties that human life contains the anxieties concerning the truth and meaningfulness of existence. Why are we here? What will become of us? What is life finally about? Is there truth that can be trusted as the child trusts the mother's breast?

While the psalm expresses humility before the great questions of the ultimate meaningfulness of things, it also may be seen to reveal the way these questions tend to be avoided. The lines "O Lord, my heart is not lifted up, my eyes are not raised too high; I do not occupy myself with things too great and too marvelous for me" seem to suggest an idealization and advocacy of a piety that submissively refuses to engage existential anxiety, that keeps its eyes turned down. Such piety never dares to shake a fist at the heavens or storm the heights of divine distance to demand answers to these imponderable questions in the manner, say, of Job. The result can be that God remains distant and the human relationship with God stays passive and deadening instead of being the lively and confronting relationship so frequently reported in the biblical texts.

Yet the ultimate questions of truth endure. Seldom stated directly as questions, rarely shared except in moments of deep personal trust and relationship, these questions persist even for the most thoroughly modern persons who have long since turned to science for the answers to most of the questions about truth. Such questions, of course, become more urgent in times of crisis, such as a life-threatening illness or the death of a loved person or important public figure. Then perhaps they will be spoken, sometimes in agonized doubt and frustrated disappointment. But most of the time they simply hover in the background unspoken or pondered in the aloneness of a dark and sleepless night.

For some the mere presence of the pastor raises these questions, though they may resist articulation for fear of the pastor's disapproval. Attitude, or an embarrassed self-consciousness at the pastor's appearance, may silently signal the suppressed wish to raise a question or share a doubtful lack of certainty concerning what the Christian story has been understood to say about these matters of ultimate truth and meaningfulness. For others, the pastor's presence signals the need to declare that all is well with one's soul. But virtually always the pastor's presence is a reminder that there are such questions and that they require consideration.

Many pastors likewise have difficulty allowing these imponderable questions to surface and find articulation. The popular cultural myth that the pastor is supposed to be the one who has the answers to questions of ultimate truth is itself intimidating. Does the pastor dare admit to facing these questions also? On the other hand, the popular culture of modernity scoffs at the supposed answers presented by the hucksters of fundamentalist folk religion that dominate the image of religion presented on radio and television. Caught between these two popular images of pastoral authority concerning ultimate truth, many pastors fall into awkward silence or the mouthing of religious clichés.

Here the model of pastoral care rooted in the biblical narrative tradition has much to offer both pastor and parishioner. Taking that narrative seriously as primary source for reflection on questions of ultimate truth opens one's awareness to the realization that these questions are in reality timeless. They appear at every level of historical development of the biblical story of the world. The narrative itself becomes in a sense the answer to our questions in that we become participants in the story and its ongoing search for truth and faithful trust in the promises of God as narrated in the story. Like the ancient patriarchs or the writers of the psalms, we can become free to speak more openly of our questions and share our humility before those questions that are "too great and too marvelous" for us.

Pastors who are seeking to guide the interpretive process of the people of God will thus be alert to signals from persons that indicate when the flow of life experience has pressed the great questions of truth upon them. Rather than too quickly speaking a word designed to bring the question to closure, these pastoral interpreters will invite further conversation, and a shared search for clarity concerning the nature of the question, and support the tentative affirmation that comes out of having faced and wrestled with the doubt and mistrust that the question expresses.

Looking back upon the sixfold typology of issues by which I have attempted to analyze the content that shapes pastoral observation and participation in the day-to-day activity of pastoral care, several things become apparent. First, these various types of issues will seldom be present in pure form. The different levels of issues will rather be most often intertwined and interlayered. Second, the entry point for interpretive pastoral conversation may lie at any of the six levels, but questions at other levels will most often be at least latently present. This means that there is no "right" point of entry and no "right" direction that hermeneutical pastoral conversation should take. Third, for the parishioner the search for resolution of issues at different levels may be intermittent and fragmentary. The flow of life experience can tend to close off exploration of a given level of question as well as open that level up to new or more urgent inquiry. The pastor needs to be both sensitive to this ebb and flow, moving as it moves, and invitingly open to a deeper and more pervasive search for clarity about the soul's issues and experiential expression of the fruits of faith.

We come now to the end of this book, in which I have attempted to develop and test a narrative hermeneutical practical theology with which to undergird the ministry of pastoral care in a time of cultural pluralism and fragmentation. I have argued that ours is a time when the horizons of pastoral care must be widened to include concern for the pain, anxiety, and confusion of purpose being experienced by ordinary people within and outside our communities of faith, when life seems no longer to cohere. While pluralism has in certain ways been salutary in that some of the reified social constructions of particularly middle-class white culture have to a considerable degree been broken open, for many the subtle and pervasive impact of pluralism has been experienced in ways that fragment taken-for-granted structures of meaning.

I have argued that the situation of pluralism can be best understood as originating in a pluralism of narrative structures, a pluralism of stories of what the world is about and what human life in the world is about. In multiple ways these differing stories of the world cut across each other and compete for the loyalty and commitment of persons. Every human activity is informed by such a story of the world and human life in the world. Ordinary folk must often move from one activity informed by its grounding story to another grounded in a very different narrative in the course of a single day. Thus pluralism of narratives impacts individual identity and purpose in ways that both create and complicate issues in the life of a given individual.

I have argued that in a culture having to adapt to this pervasive impact of pluralism it is impossible, even undesirable, to attempt a return to some imagined more simple time when life was held together by a single narrative structure, a single vision of what life in the world is and should be. Rather there need to be found ways in which differing narratives and their metaphors and values, their distinctive ways of seeing and interpreting things in the world, may become mutually critical of each other. By bringing differing horizons of understanding of life in the world into mutually critical proximity, a "fusion of horizons" may take place which embodies a fresh and clear vision of what life in the world is and, more important, should be.

While I have argued for the necessity of coming to terms with the continuing impact and presence of a pluralism of narratives in the modern world, I have also argued for the centrality and salvific power of the Christian story as the story of God and the people of God. It is that story within which, for Christians, all other stories of our lives need finally to be nested. And it is against that story and its root metaphors that all other narrative structures of reality need to be tested and critically evaluated. Because that story is a story of the living God who continues to act to bring about the fulfillment of God's promise for all creation, it is within the plot of that story that we who are Christians finally ground our hope for life's continuing transformation. Even so, this primary narrative structure for Christian life must itself be continually put at risk in the mutually critical correlation of its meanings with those coming from other narratives, other ways of seeing the world. For pastors and lay Christians alike, this process of mutually critical correlation engages us in a continuing formal and informal task of "practical theological thinking and reflection" on the day-to-day and week-to-week flow of human events and activities.

Finally, I have argued that this way of seeing the present

situation of Christians in a pluralistic world sets an agenda of concern and activity for the Christian pastor as he or she goes about the daily rounds of pastoral care ministry in the Christian community and in the larger community within which it is set. The fulfillment of the pastoral calling thus involves not simply the exercise of care and concern for the people of God as they experience the personal, relational, and existential crises of living which have been the focus of attention of pastoral care literature in recent years. It also means the exercise of care and concern for God's people as they seek to live their lives as participants in a pluralistic, complex world set in the flow of change within time and history.

Like life itself, the work of pastoral care is set within the flow of time. This means that the emphases of pastoral care ministry must change in response to the changing needs of persons whose lives reflect the changes of time. Yet pastoral care, if it is to remain pastoral, must retain a deep continuity with the Christian narrative tradition from which it received its primary identification. It is by sensitive interpretation and reinterpretation of both the changing situations of life and of the grounding stories of the pastoral tradition that the horizons of pastoral work are faithfully and responsively maintained. It is in being true to that task that the pastor finds fulfillment of the pastoral vocation.

Epilogue
Some Implications of Widened Horizons

Books about widened horizons should be neither written nor read as the final word about the subject that has been considered. That is true not only because efforts to widen horizons always mean exploration of new and therefore inherently tentative possibilities, but also because the very notion of widened horizons implies an ongoing process that should never be allowed to become static, as if completed. Efforts to widen horizons also inevitably leave some loose ends, topics and subtopics that have not been fully examined, implications of what has been proposed that have not been fully developed. I am thus left at the end of the writing with a number of issues, questions, and unexplored topics that call for further study, not only my own, but that of others who may bring somewhat different horizons of experience and perspective to the work. In the spirit of inviting that collaborative effort and continuing dialogue, let me then share the following afterthoughts:

1. At the level of the current theoretical/theological discussion of the meaning and basis of practical theology, there are a veritable nest of issues and problems having to do with the limits and possibilities of the narrative approach to practical pastoral theology that demand further exploration.

Several such issues have a certain empirical cast to them. Careful empirical studies that seek both to verify and to detail the manner in which deep narrative structures shape and inform the interpretive life of persons at all levels of sophistication could and should be undertaken. So-called "clinical" evidence for the presence and power of stories of the self and of the world seems to me both plentiful and readily apparent. More carefully constructed scientific empirical studies of these phenomena seem both desirable and possible. These studies should not be left simply to the social scientists, however. Pastors and pastoral theologians with the requisite scientific expertise and interest can contribute significantly to those efforts to the benefit of both the social scientific community and the church.

Important as empirical studies are, my own background and penchant lead me to look in a somewhat different direction for further exploration of the possibilities of the narrative paradigm. In a time of cultural fragmentation and transition, I am deeply interested in doing further work in probing the biblical images and metaphorical resources that may offer those of us in the West a way through the cultural malaise with which we are afflicted. In a time such as ours the search for richer, more liberating, and comprehensive images to inform the goals and purposes toward which our efforts in living may be directed needs to be informed by metaphors and narrative themes that transcend our immediate cultural situation. Both as a contribution to that cultural search for situation-transcendent roots and because of the identity we claim as the people of God, the shared praxis of the Christian life needs desperately to reappropriate the central images of our tradition in ways that may rescue us from both the banality of many of our models of Christian community and the too-easy narrow individualism of the appropriation of the faith by many Protestant Christians of our time.

I would like to explore further just what it means for ordinary folk to have a Christian vocation in the workaday world. Just what does the image of "presence," whether that refer to the presence of God or the presence of the Christian in the world, mean in relation to that mundane world of human affairs? In reference to God, that image of presence is, in the biblical tradition, always in tension with the image of God's absence—the mystery of God's elusive presence.[1] What does it mean to live as a child of the covenant in the modern world? These and other questions that significantly relate to the goals toward which our pastoral work should be directed beckon for further study. The link between *pastoral* care and the deepest narrative sources of our tradition necessitates further research in relation to this important set of issues and hermeneutical problems. Lest that research unwittingly remain too narrowly culturally bound by Western middle-class perspectives, it needs ideally to involve collaboration with persons from other parts of the world, other socially constructed perspectives on what the "real" world is like.

The relationship between the narrative hermeneutical approach set forth on these pages and the grounding of practical pastoral theology in theological ethics presented by such pastoral theologians as Don S. Browning likewise needs to be further explored. Browning's proposal fundamentally grounds practical theological thinking in human obligational relationships, though he acknowledges the underlying mythic structures that lie behind all modes of obligational ethical thinking. The approach set forth here, on the other hand, recognizes the importance of normative structures of obligation, but it grounds practical pastoral theology in narrative in at least two ways that go beyond Browning's acknowledgment of its importance. First, at the level of human interpretive experience, my understanding is that humans tend to make what may be seen externally as moral decisions more on the basis of characteristic modes of interpretation of what is going on in their narratively constructed world than on grounds of what can legitimately be called "moral reasoning," even though moral reasoning may at times be involved. Choices and decisions are therefore informed more fundamentally by levels of human experience that are at their deepest level metaphorical—that is, imagistic, symbolic, and affective—rather than by reason.

Second, at the level of fundamental narrative theology, the approach taken here is unabashedly confessional at the point of expressing confidence in the presence and power of God in the movement of events and relationships in time and history. Christian narrative practical theology is finally grounded in the ongoing praxis of God as God acts to fulfill God's promise for creation. Practical pastoral theological thinking is therefore not simply concerned with what is obligative for a given situation, normatively speaking, but with human action in response to the actions of God.

2. Having said the foregoing, I need to acknowledge that there remains a problem for a narrative metaphorical approach to practical pastoral theology at the point of the paradoxical tension between what in my earlier hermeneutical study of pastoral counseling I called, following Paul Ricoeur, the tension between a language of force and a language of meaning.[2] This problem might well be called the problem of the limits of narrative. Humans make interpretations of all manner of events and relationships based on their stories of self and world. But in every event, every relationship, there is involved a certain hard facticity, a certain forceful presence of what actually occurs. Forces, both internal to the person or community and external to them, act to bring things about. In a sense, the human struggle for meaning

is a struggle to humanize events and forces that shape human destiny, just as I have said earlier that narratives are the human effort to humanize time. Thus our stories always function within the limits of what is not shaped by story. Just how these two realities—force and meaning—are related in the shaping of human presence and movement in the world remains a stubborn problem demanding further examination from a variety of perspectives beyond the scope of the present work.

3. At the level of specific concern for competent and relevant ministry there are several issues, problems, and possibilities that call for further work related to the quest for a unified and coherent theory of ministry. The narrative hermeneutical approach to practical theology has much to offer by way of providing a basis for achieving greater unity and coherence for all aspects of the parish pastoral role. If, as I have argued, practical theological thinking can best be undertaken in a narrative hermeneutical mode, it may logically be concluded that the possibilities for a unified theory to undergird ministry practice in all roles of ministry, including preaching, education, liturgical, organizational and administrative leadership, mission, and outreach, are best found in considering each of these roles from a narrative hermeneutical perspective. Yet the specific implications of such a proposal call for much more careful development than the scope of the present book has permitted.

Clearly the role of the pastor as interpretive guide can be fulfilled in a wide range of relational contexts. In both formal and informal groups where issues of Christian living are being discussed, the pastor's guidance role is both crucial and challenging. Much good preaching that relates biblical images and themes to contemporary life situations is an expression of the pastor's role as interpretive guide. Likewise leadership of the congregation in its mission efforts and its organizational activities continually involves the pastor in the interpretation of the faith as expressed in the life of the congregation and its ministry.

Such a proposal as this calls for collaborative research in the form of careful experimentation and collection of concrete data by means of case studies, logs of recorded experience, and the like on the part of practicing pastors of churches who must perform all these varied roles of parish ministry. It also calls for collaborative study and dialogue with specialists in the practical disciplines of ministry other than pastoral care. One of the more promising outcomes of the resurgent interest in practical theology lies in the possibility it offers for providing a basis for unity among the ministerial disciplines, both functional and theological/ethical. The argument of this book assumes the desirability of further collaborative efforts to mine the resources of narrative theology for undergirding practical theological inquiry in relation to all disciplines of ministry.

4. Finally, my own vocational location dictates that I not end this short excursus on possibilities and issues yet to be more fully explored without making brief reference to the implications of the argument of this book for theological education, both at the level of basic ministry studies in preparation for professional ministry and at the level of the pastor's continuing education. Assuming that among my readers will probably be found both seminarians and practicing pastors searching for insights to guide their ministry efforts, I will be bold to share two suggestive ideas which beg for further development and experimentation.

First, theological education in preparation for ministry has, in my view, tended to be modeled too woodenly on two educational paradigms found in Western culture: namely, those of the liberal arts curriculum and of the forms and educational practices of the specialized disciplines. Following the liberal arts paradigm, basic theological education has required introductory-level course work in a variety of fields thought to provide important background knowledge and perspectives pertinent to ministry practice. Thus students are introduced to church history, historical-critical studies of the Bible, systematic theology, ethics, sociology of religion, and the like, each taught by specialists in those fields. They are also exposed to introductory courses in pastoral care, Christian education, church administration, and evangelism, each again taught by specialists in those several so-called praxis disciplines.

In various ways different theological schools have attempted to assist students to "integrate" the knowledge they have gained through these various introductory specialized courses and relate that integrated perspective to the broad scope of ministry practice in the contemporary sociocultural situation. Considerable progress has been made over the last twenty years or so in building so-called contextual education programs into that mix of specialized and integrative educational experiences.

The stubbornly persistent problem for theological education at the preparatory level is that the students, while gaining an introductory level of knowledge (often spoken of as a "smattering") of the variety of specialized fields pertinent to ministry studies, fail to achieve an ability to integrate what they have been taught into a holistic perspective that can be brought to bear on concrete personal, social, and existential problems confronting the church in the contemporary world. This failure is most often spoken of by their teachers as an "inability to think theologically about present-day issues." Even those who can do this level of integrative thinking tend to have difficulty at the point of exercising the practical knowledge, wise judgment, and leadership skills essential for ministry to and with congregations.

The suggestion concerning the problem of preparatory theological education which the work of this book has brought to the fore in my thinking about the problem has to do with the possibility of rethinking both the content and sequencing of ministry studies around the image of the preparation of the pastor for the role I have here called that of the interpretive guide in the community of the people of God. I am intrigued with the possibilities that might open if that image became, as it were, an extended metaphor around which the preparation of seminarians for ministry is to be organized.

The scenario that emerges begins with the early introduction of the student to the centrality of this role in ministry and the introduction of the problem of interpretation of both traditional sources for Christian interpretation (biblical, historical, and theological) and the problem of interpretation of present-day human situations that call forth the ministry of the church. The deepening and enlarging of skills in both these levels of interpretation would, in that scenario, become the organizing theme around which ministry studies would be sequenced and the student's own sense of maturing ministry competence developed.

Central to that organizational metaphor would be the rethinking of course content in specific ways to assist the student to become skilled in what I have termed, following David Tracy, the mutually critical correlation of perspectives. Students would be expected to attain a degree of knowledge and competence in bringing to bear a variety of disciplinary perspectives, including biblical, theological/ethical, social scientific, narrative/hermeneutical, historical, and operational/practical on a wide variety of concrete problems of contemporary life. Contextual education activities would be designed to call forth these skills in a variety of actual situations of ministry.

Second, the proposal I have made in this book likewise suggests possibilities for both the structure and content of continuing education for practicing parish pastors. It would certainly suggest to pastor readers that they look for continuing education experiences that seem to offer opportunities for enlarging and enriching their knowledge and skills in the art of interpretation, both in relation to the sources of the Christian narrative faith and in relation to situations of modern life. Opportunities to think deeply about actual case studies in one's ministry, making use of the schemas set forth in this book or comparable schemas that sharpen and increase one's skill in doing practical theological thinking, seem clearly to offer the greatest possibility of renewing one's preparation for the ministry of interpretive guidance. Exposures to perspectives on present-day cultural problems coming from nontheological disciplines such as cultural anthropology, sociology of knowledge, psychoanalytic and systems psychologies, and the like can also enrich the pastor's capacities for doing the work of mutually critical correlation of these perspectives with those of Christian theology.

These and other afterthoughts preoccupy me as I bring this study to a close. The narrative hermeneutical process continues to beckon. The work of practical theological thinking does not end—for me, as, I hope, it does not for the reader.

Notes

Introduction: Widening Horizons by Redefining the Task

1. "A central thesis then begins to emerge: man is in his actions and practice, as well as in his fictions, essentially a story-telling animal. He is not essentially, but becomes through his history, a teller of stories that aspire to truth. But the key question for men is not about their own authorship; I can only answer the question 'What am I to do?' if I can answer the prior question 'Of what story or stories do I find myself a part?' . . . Hence there is no way to give us an understanding of any society including our own, except through the stock of stories which constitute its initial dramatic resources. Mythology, in its original sense, is at the heart of things" (Alasdair MacIntyre, *After Virtue* [Notre Dame, Ind.: University of Notre Dame Press, 1981], p. 201).

2. For a rich and provocative analysis of the shifts that have taken place in ways of thinking and acting pastorally in relation to perceived human needs and problems in American history, see E. Brooks Holifield, *A History of Pastoral Care in America* (Nashville: Abingdon Press, 1983).

3. Ibid., p. 260.

4. Consider, for example, the great influence the ideas concerning the care of the dying popularized by the compassionate psychiatrist, Elisabeth Kübler-Ross, have had on what is considered appropriate pastoral care of such persons. So-called "stages of dying" theories presuppose a notion that dying is best interpreted as a "normal," if final, stage in human growth through which the individual should be helped to realize whatever integrity and fulfillment is possible. At least in the beginning of pastoral appropriation of that way of seeing death experience, corporate groups such as families or hospital staffs were often seen as interfering with that final process of self-realization. More recently the interpretations of dying originating with Kübler-Ross have virtually become normative for the practice of care of the dying by many hospital staffs.

5. The pastoral theologian who has been most articulate concerning the changed sociocultural situation is undoubtedly Don S. Browning.

His book *The Moral Context of Pastoral Care* (Philadelphia: Westminster Press, 1976), presents a detailed and clarifying analysis of the changed context in which pastoral care ministry must take place. Browning's major observation is that, because of the impact of rapid social change, pluralism in values and morals, and the resulting confusion concerning the nature of the good, there has developed a situation in Western culture best described as a loss of a consensual moral context. The modes of pastoral care of the recent past have, says Browning, assumed the existence of a taken-for-granted moral context to which the person seeking forgiving, accepting care would return. Temporarily the moral sanctions of that context could be "bracketed" and the caring situation be governed by an ethic of forgiveness and accepting restoration. Now, however, that consensual moral context has been lost to a fragmentation of values and moral strictures on self and group behavior, thus creating a new context and an altered task for pastoral care ministry.

I also have in mind here such social critics as sociologist Peter L. Berger (*Facing Up to Modernity* [New York: Basic Books, 1977] and, with Brigitte Berger and Hansfield Kellner, *The Homeless Mind* [New York: Random House, 1973]) and social psychologist Richard Sennett (*The Fall of Public Man* [New York: Alfred A. Knopf, 1977] and *Authority* [New York: Random House, Vintage Books, 1981]).

Don Browning, in *The Moral Context of Pastoral Care*, proposes a direction for pastoral care practice governed by "moral inquiry," a concept he develops more systematically as "practical moral reasoning" in his later *Religious Ethics and Pastoral Care* (Philadelphia: Fortress Press, 1983). The similarities and differences between Browning's proposal and that herein developed will become apparent later.

6. The term *tribalism* is one used by a number of social scientists to point to the phenomenon most clearly apparent among people of common ethnic or other social background who have been geographically or culturally displaced from familiar surroundings. My own use of the term has been informed most significantly by the work of British sociologist Peter Marris, in his book *Loss and Change* (New York: Random House, Pantheon Books, 1974).

7. "Modern identity is *peculiarly differentiated.* Because of the plurality of social worlds in modern society, the structures of each particular world are experienced as relatively unstable and unreliable. The individual in most pre-modern societies lives in a world that is much more coherent. It therefore appears to him as firm and possibly inevitable. By contrast, the modern individual's experience of a plurality of social worlds relativizes every one of them. Consequently, the institutional order undergoes a certain loss of reality. The 'accent of reality' consequently shifts from the objective order of institutions to the realm of subjectivity. Put differently, the individual's experience of himself becomes more real to him than his experience of the objective social world. Therefore, the individual seeks to find his 'foothold' in reality in himself rather than outside himself. One consequence of this is that the individual's subjective reality (what is commonly regarded as his

'psychology') becomes increasingly differentiated, complex—and 'interesting' to himself. Subjectivity acquires previously unconceived 'depths.' " Berger, Berger, and Kellner, *The Homeless Mind*, pp. 77 and 78.

8. Heinz Kohut, *The Restoration of the Self* (New York: International Universities Press, 1977), p. 133. For a brief but more elaborate account of Kohut's thought than space or purpose permit here, see my *The Living Human Document* (Nashville: Abingdon Press, 1984), pp. 91, 92, 93.

9. H. Richard Niebuhr, *The Responsible Self* (New York: Harper & Row, 1963).

10. Ibid., pp. 61, 62, 63, 64, 65.

11. Ibid., pp. 124, 126.

Chapter 1: Story and Goal: Christian Life in the Modern World

1. James B. Wiggins, ed., *Religion as Story* (New York: Harper & Row, 1975), p. 30.

2. Brian Wicker, *The Story-shaped World: Fiction and Metaphysics: Some Variations on a Theme* (Notre Dame, Ind.: University of Notre Dame Press, 1975), p. 4.

3. Ibid., p. 7.

4. Charles E. Reagan and David Stewart, eds., *The Philosophy of Paul Ricoeur* (Boston: Beacon Press, 1978), p. 169.

5. Barbara Hardy, as quoted in Wicker, *The Story-shaped World*, p. 47.

6. Paul Ricoeur, *Time and Narrative* vol. 1 (Chicago: University of Chicago Press, 1984), p. 52. See also Alasdair MacIntyre, *After Virtue* (Notre Dame, Ind.: University of Notre Dame Press, 1981), p. 197.

7. Robert N. Bellah, Richard Madsen, William M. Sullivan, Ann Swidler, and Steven M. Tipton, *Habits of the Heart: Individualism and Commitment in American Life* (Berkeley, Calif.: University of California Press, 1985), p. 302.

8. See Northrop Frye, *The Educated Imagination* (Bloomington, Ind.: Indiana University Press, 1964), p. 110.

9. I was first introduced to the notion of a broken connection between present lived experience and the grounding narrative images and metaphors by the psychiatrist Robert Jay Lifton. In his book titled *The Broken Connection* (New York: Simon & Schuster, 1979), Lifton develops this notion particularly in relation to the impact of the nuclear age on historic narrative images of immortality and transcendence. See especially chapters 19 and 20 of that book for Lifton's explication of his use of the "broken connection" phrase.

10. See Philip Greven, *The Protestant Temperament: Patterns of Child-rearing, Religious Experience, and the Self in Early America* (New York: Alfred A. Knopf, 1978).

11. David Kantor and William Lehr, *Inside the Family* (San Francisco: Jossey-Bass, 1975).

12. Charles Y. Glock and Robert N. Bellah, eds., *The New Religious Consciousness* (Berkeley, Calif: University of California Press, 1976), pp. 234, 235.

13. Robert N. Bellah, *The Broken Covenant: American Civil Religion in a Time of Trial* (New York: Seabury Press, 1975).

14. Glock and Bellah, *The New Religious Consciousness*, p. 335. It should also be noted that in the more recent study of patterns of moral decision making reported by Bellah and his associates in the book *Habits of the Heart*, the theme of conflict between individualism and biblically grounded covenant life in American cultural history is continued.

15. Max Weber, *The Protestant Ethic and the Spirit of Capitalism* (New York: Seabury Press, 1958).

For an interesting and wide-ranging discussion of the tension between individualism and modern corporate American control in politics and business, see Peter L. Berger, *Facing Up to Modernity* (New York: Basic Books, 1979). Berger's comments on pages 36 and 37 are particularly pertinent to my reference here to Max Weber.

16. For a clarifying discussion of live and dead metaphors, see Sallie McFague, *Metaphorical Theology: Models of God in Religious Language* (Philadelphia: Fortress Press, 1982). McFague would suggest that the lively use of the affirmation concerning the faithfulness of God by my remembered black women is dependent upon a certain retention of the "is and is not" quality of the affirmation. The "How long, O Lord?" question contains both the is and is not of the metaphor and thus it retains its vitality. Spoken as a literal pious statement it threatens to become so literalized and trivial as to become dead. See pages 37 and 38. See also Paul Ricoeur, *The Rule of Metaphor: Multi-disciplinary Studies of the Creation of Meaning in Language* (Toronto: University of Toronto Press, 1981), p. 99.

17. Jürgen Moltmann, *The Church in the Power of the Spirit* (New York: Harper & Row, 1977), p. 22. See also my *The Living Human Document* (Nashville: Abingdon Press, 1984), pp. 67, 68, 69, 70.

18. It needs perhaps to be stated here that the process of maintaining a connection between present experience and deep narrative metaphorical themes is not entirely or even primarily a conscious, intellectual process. Rather it involves the deeper layers of emotional and affectional involvement in a community that incorporates the language and meanings of those metaphorical themes, celebrates its connection with those meanings, and signifies for the individual his or her involvement in them.

19. Joseph L. Allen, *Love and Conflict: A Covenantal Model of Christian Ethics* (Nashville: Abingdon Press, 1984), pp. 39, 40.

20. Ricoeur, *Time and Narrative*, p. 60.

Chapter 2: Stories and *The Story:* Narrative Theology and the Task of Pastoral Care

1. Michael Goldberg, *Theology and Narrative: A Critical Introduction* (Nashville: Abingdon Press, 1982), ch. 5. The typology is summarized on page 155.

2. Hans Frei, *The Eclipse of Biblical Narrative* (New Haven: Yale University Press, 1974).

3. Sallie McFague, *Speaking in Parables: A Study in Metaphor and Theology* (Philadelphia: Fortress Press, 1975).

4. Goldberg, *Theology and Narrative*, p. 156.

5. Ibid., p. 160.

6. Ibid., p. 162.

7. For a less technical and therefore in certain ways more accessibly inviting explication of the approach to biblical narrative taken by Hans Frei, see the short introductory essay, "A Single Meaning: Notes on the Origins and Life of Narrative," in Reynolds Price, *A Palpable God* (New York: Atheneum Publishers, 1978).

8. McFague, *Speaking in Parables*, p. 76.

9. Sallie McFague, *Metaphorical Theology: Models of God in Religious Language* (Philadelphia: Fortress Press, 1982), p. 134. McFague here follows the analysis of metaphor given by Paul Ricoeur. See his *The Rule of Metaphor: Multi-disciplinary Studies of the Creation of Meaning in Language* (Toronto: University of Toronto Press, 1981), pp. 255, 256.

10. Paul van Buren, *The Burden of Freedom: Americans and the God of Israel* (New York: Seabury Press, 1976) and *Discerning the Way* (New York: Seabury Press, 1980).

11. Irving Greenberg, "Judaism and History: Historical Events and Religious Change," in *Perspectives in Jewish Learning*, vol. 1, ed. by Stanley Kazan and Nathaniel Stampfer (Chicago: Spertus College Press, 1977).

12. Goldberg, *Theology and Narrative*, pp. 165–168.

13. Ibid., p. 170.

14. Stanley Hauerwas, *Vision and Virtue: Essays in Christian Ethical Reflection* (Notre Dame, Ind.: Fides Publishers, 1974).

15. Ibid., p. 29.

16. Ibid., p. 71.

17. McFague, *Metaphorical Theology*, p. 54.

18. Readers who have followed the development of the author's thought concerning the theological framework for pastoral theology to be found in the trinitarian theology of Jürgen Moltmann may be interested to note that my interpretation of Moltmann's theology is fundamentally a narrative interpretation. As Moltmann formulates his trinitarian theology, the trinitarian imagery is essentially imagery of the story of the life of God within the ecology of God's internal relationships and in the plurality of God's relationships to the world. He bases this trinitarian narrative of God in the biblical story of the cross and resurrection. Thus Moltmann's theology is genuinely a narrative theology. See especially Jürgen Moltmann, *The Crucified God* (New York: Harper & Row, 1974) and *The Trinity and the Kingdom* (San Francisco: Harper & Row, 1981). Cf. my *The Living Human Document* (Nashville: Abingdon Press, 1984), pp. 66–71, 111, 112. Cf. also George A. Lindbeck, *The Nature of Doctrine: Religion and Theology in a Postliberal Age* (Philadelphia: Westminster Press, 1984), especially ch. 6.

19. Paul Ricoeur, *Time and Narrative*, vol. 1 (Chicago: University of Chicago Press, 1984), p. 52.

20. For a concise history of this philosophical tradition, see Richard Palmer, *Hermeneutics* (Evanston, Ill.: Northwestern University Press, 1969).

21. Ricoeur, *Time and Narrative*, p. 60.

22. Gerkin, *The Living Human Document*. See particularly chapters 4 and 5 for the psychological grounding for the notion of narrative as the human structuring of time.

23. H. Richard Niebuhr, "War as the Judgment of God," *The Christian Century*, vol. 59 (1942), p. 630, as quoted in James M. Gustafson, *Can Ethics Be Christian?* (Chicago: University of Chicago Press, 1975), p. 125.

24. Peter L. Berger and Thomas Luckmann, *The Social Construction of Reality* (Garden City, N.Y.: Doubleday & Co., Anchor Books, 1967), p. 23.

25. H. Richard Niebuhr, *The Meaning of Revelation* (New York: Macmillan Co., 1941), p. 101.

26. Ibid., p. 102.

27. Gustafson, *Can Ethics Be Christian?* p. 69.

Chapter 3: The Structure: Elements of a Hermeneutical Theory of Practical Theology

1. The phrase "theory of practical theology" is an ambiguous phrase that mixes together the two terms, "theory" and "praxis," which, in recent times at least, have often been separated (as in the notion of praxis as applied theory). My purpose is not to formulate a theory that can then be applied, but rather to unravel insofar as possible a mode of practical hermeneutical thinking which is at the same time both immersed in praxis and attentive to issues of theory and theology that emerge from arenas beyond the immediate situation of praxis.

2. Don S. Browning, *Practical Theology: The Emerging Field in Theology, Church, and World* (San Francisco: Harper & Row, 1983), p. 149.

3. The concept of the fusion of horizons of meaning is taken from the work of the hermeneutical philosopher Hans-Georg Gadamer. See his *Truth and Method* (New York: Seabury Press, 1975), pp. 269–274, for his explication of that concept. See also my *The Living Human Document*, (Nashville: Abingdon Press, 1984) pp. 44–47 and 137, for the implications of the concept for pastoral counseling. The concept is important in the present context because it is suggestive of the manner in which the horizon of meaning shaped by the Christian narrative of the world must be brought into dialogical conversation with the horizons represented in other ways of seeing the world embodied in the narratives that inform the many activities in which Christians become involved in modern life. It is in the process of dialogical fusion of these differing horizons that a fresh perspective on the activity at hand may emerge that takes seriously both the Christian horizon and the horizon present in the activity, while in a sense creating a truly new horizon, a new way of seeing the situation at hand, out of the fusion. Cf. Thomas W. Ogletree,

Hospitality to the Stranger (Philadelphia: Fortress Press, 1985), pp. 120, 121.

4. The phrase "mutually critical correlation" is taken from the theologian David Tracy. For a summary of his understanding of the concept see his essay in the Browning book *Practical Theology* titled "The Foundations of Practical Theology." Tracy there defines theology as "the mutually critical correlation of the meaning and truth of an interpretation of the Christian fact and the meaning and truth of an interpretation of the contemporary situation" (p. 65). See also his *The Blessed Rage for Order* (New York: Seabury Press, Crossroad Book, 1975). For a helpful critique of the approach to theology taken by David Tracy, see George A. Lindbeck, *The Nature of Doctrine: Religion and Theology in a Postliberal Age* (Philadelphia: Westminster Press, 1984). Lindbeck's critique involves his classification of theological systems as having in general one of three approaches to their formation: propositional, experiental-expressive, or cultural-linguistic. Both propositional and experiential-expressive types are "extratextual" in their formation. In either case the system "locates religious meaning outside the text or semiotic system either in the objective realities to which it refers or in the experiences it symbolizes, whereas for cultural-linguists the meaning is immanent. Meaning is constituted by the uses of a specific language rather than being distinguishable from it. Thus the proper way to determine what 'God' signifies for example, is by examining how the word operates within a religion and thereby shapes reality and experience rather than by first establishing its propositional or experiential meaning and reinterpreting or reformulating its uses accordingly" (p. 114). Lindbeck classifies Tracy's approach as experiential-expressive rather than as intratextual and argues for a more clearly "cultural-linguistic" approach as a way of coming to grips with the particularity of Christian scriptural sources rather than an approach to scripture as "classic" text as does Tracy. Although Lindbeck's argument seems to this writer to be in certain ways useful, it does not appear to take the necessity of interdisciplinary dialogue seriously enough as does Tracy. From my perspective it is clearly not possible to account for all truth from within one narrative language system. Thus interdisciplinary dialogue and mutually critical correlation of differing language perspectives is necessary. At the same time, like Lindbeck I wish to preserve the primacy of a grounding cultural "intratextual" language. This perhaps suggests that the position here taken is one that attempts to bridge the gap between what Lindbeck calls "experiential-expressive" and "cultural-linguistic" approaches to theological thinking. In any case, Lindbeck's argument does not seem to undercut the validity of Tracy's approach to "mutually critical correlation."

5. The phrase "hermeneutic of suspicion" is here taken, following Paul Ricoeur, to mean the expectation that all ways of interpreting and seeing involve a degree of false-consciousness or hidden self-interest. See Charles E. Reagan and David Stewart, eds., *The Philosophy of Paul Ricoeur* (Boston: Beacon Press, 1978), pp. 214, 215.

6. For a more extended discussion of the problem of the interplay of force and meaning in the shaping of human behavior and response, see my *The Living Human Document*, pp. 39–40, 50, 103, 192.

7. My understanding of this tension has recently been greatly assisted by two essays in the Browning collection referred to in note 2 of this chapter. Dennis McCann, in his article "Practical Theology and Social Action: Or, What Can the 1980's Learn from the 1960's?" makes use of a concept drawn from J. H. Oldham and John C. Bennett termed "middle axioms." "Middle axioms, as Oldham insists, are meant 'to discern the signs of the times' or, in Bennett's words, they 'guide us in determining the goals which represent the purpose of God for our time.' . . . Middle axioms help to overcome the 'distance' betweeen 'our best achievements' and the 'fulness' of the Kingdom of God" (Browning, p. 115).

The other essay, by James Lapsley, is "Practical Theology and Pastoral Care: An Essay in Pastoral Theology." Here Lapsley takes his editor, Don Browning, to task for his effort to construct a theory of pastoral care as a branch of theological ethics. While acknowledging that normative ethical issues are indeed encountered regularly in pastoral care situations, Lapsley declares that there must be involved in pastoral care the scrutiny of other data that arise from being in the actual situation with real persons in concrete human relationships. "It is this grubbing in the root systems of human need and human hope with the intent to strengthen, nurture, and, if possible, to aid development that provides the particularity of pastoral theology, and it is the source of its potential and actual contributions to theology" (Browning, p. 171). Lapsley goes on to suggest that it is in the discernment of possibilities that pastoral theological thinking may do its best work.

8. Here I am drawing not only on the theology of H. Richard Niebuhr but on that of Jürgen Moltmann and Wolfhart Pannenberg as well. While Niebuhr's concept, referred to earlier, having to do with our human response to the actions of others in our present situation needing to be as to the action of God is important from an ethical perspective, it does not, in my view, take seriously enough our dependence upon the activity of the Spirit. For Pannenberg the power of God in God's activity is the Power of the future God is bringing about. That Power comes toward us in every situation seeking to lure us out of our present situation into the future of God. (Wolfhart Pannenberg, *Theology and the Kingdom of God* [Philadelphia: Westminster Press, 1969], pp. 53–56.)

Moltmann's theology of the Spirit is central to my thought here also, since for Moltmann it is by the power of the Spirit that God works "to make the impossible possible; he creates faith where there is nothing to believe in; he creates love where there is nothing lovable; he creates hope where there is nothing to hope for." The Spirit thus "wakes sleeping, suppressed or otherwise imprisoned potentialities and activates them for the divine rule." (Jürgen Moltmann, *The Church in the Power of the Spirit* [New York: Harper & Row, 1977], p. 191.)

Chapter 4: Testing the Structure: The Case of Centerton

1. The value, for example, of such social scientific studies of small communities as that of Arthur Vidich and Joseph Bensman (*Small Town in Mass Society: Class, Power and Religion in a Rural Community* [Princeton, N.J.: Princeton University Press, 1958]) to assist the pastor of the Centerton church in understanding what is going on in that situation is readily apparent. Pastors may without undue research collect important statistical and sociological data about the communities in which their ministries are located. While useful, this form of "on the spot" research does not negate, but rather complements the perspective gained from narrative inquiry such as I am here emphasizing.

2. For a penetrating and cogent analysis of the difficulties involved in uncovering actual historical facticity concerning any historical process, see Donald P. Spence, *Narrative Truth and Historical Truth: Meaning and Interpretation in Psychoanalysis* (New York: W. W. Norton & Co,. 1982).

3. For an excellent model of congregational or group reflection on the Christian tradition and its story in relation to contemporary experience, see James D. Whitehead and Evelyn E. Whitehead, *Method in Ministry: Theological Reflection and Christian Ministry* (New York: Seabury Press, 1980). Chapter 2 of that work is particularly pertinent to my purpose here.

4. Cf. Walter Brueggemann, *The Prophetic Imagination* (Philadelphia: Fortress Press, 1978), ch. 4.

5. Richard Sennett, *Authority* (New York: Random House, Vintage Books, 1981), ch. 2.

6. Full discussion of differing ways in which moral/ethical reflection might be undertaken in this case is not possible within the space limits of this chapter. For a very detailed and sophisticated presentation of a predominantly ethical approach to analysis of cases such as this one that is in certain respects closely related to the approach here taken, see Don S. Browning, *Religious Ethics and Pastoral Care* (Philadelphia: Fortress Press, 1983), especially chs. 5, 6, and 7. Cf. also Stanley Hauerwas, *Vision and Virtue: Essays in Christian Ethical Reflection* (Notre Dame, Ind.: Fides Publishers, 1974), chs. 3 and 4, and, by the same author, *Character and the Christian Life: A Study in Theological Ethics* (San Antonio: Trinity University Press, 1975), ch. 3.

7. See note 7, chapter 3, above.

8. Abraham Heschel, *The Prophets*, vol. 1 (New York: Harper & Row. Harper Torchbooks, 1969), p. 6.

9. Seward Hiltner, *Preface to Pastoral Theology* (Nashville: Abingdon Press, 1958).

10. The work of Donald Capps in relation to pastoral hermeneutics makes a helpful contribution at this point. While Capps's work is somewhat parallel to and complementary to my own, his starting point for hermeneutical reflection on situations evoking pastoral care is different. Capps begins, as I do, with the notion that human actions may be "read" as "texts" to be interpreted. Capps, however, begins his consideration of the implications of this notion for pastoral care with the implication that

pastoral actions "disclose a world." Implicit in any pastoral act therefore is the disclosure of a world that either is or is not inhabited by images of a world of faith. Evaluative assessment of pastoral acts can therefore be undertaken by means of a hermeneutical model "that seeks to gain insight into the meaning of such pastoral actions (by addressing) itself to three factors, with each building on the previous one in an essentially circular process: (1) identifying the basic *dynamic* of the pastoral action; (2) making a *diagnostic* assessment of the action; and (3) determining whether and in what ways the action is *disclosive*." (Donald Capps, *Pastoral Care and Hermeneutics* [Philadelphia: Fortress Press, 1984], p. 49.)

While I value Donald Capps's contribution to our understanding of how pastoral actions may disclose a world of faith in their implicit meanings, I believe the process of hermeneutical reflection needs to begin with consideration of the meaning worlds disclosed in the talk, the actions, and the relationships of those persons toward whom pastoral care is to be directed. Accurate and rich perception of those meaning worlds is primary in that meaningful pastoral care is always first and foremost a response to a situation of human need that evokes care. Entering into the "world" of that situation is the necessary first step.

Chapter 5: The Pastoral Task: Guiding the Interpretive Process

1. John T. McNeill, *A History of the Cure of Souls* (New York: Harper & Brothers, 1951), ch. 4.

2. William A. Clebsch and Charles R. Jaekle, *Pastoral Care in Historical Perspective* (Englewood Cliffs, N. J.: Prentice-Hall, 1964), Part 3.

3. Ibid., pp. 30, 31.

4. Walther Eichrodt, *Theology of the Old Testament*, vol. 1 (Philadelphia: Westminster Press, 1961), p. 438.

5. Abraham Heschel, *The Prophets*, vol. 2 (New York: Harper & Row, Harper Torchbooks, 1975), pp. 254–262.

6. Ibid., p. 251.

7. Charles V. Gerkin, *The Living Human Document* (Nashville: Abingdon Press, 1984), ch. 5.

8. Readers may be interested in comparing the schema given here with the results of research done by Robert Bellah and his associates on the meaning of love and marriage in American culture. See their report of that research in Robert N. Bellah, Richard Madsen, William M. Sullivan, Ann Swidler, and Steven M. Tipton, *Habits of the Heart: Individualism and Commitment in American Life* (Berkeley, Calif.: University of California Press, 1985), ch. 4.

Epilogue: Some Implications of Widened Horizons

1. Samuel Terrien, *The Elusive Presence* (San Francisco: Harper & Row, 1978).

2. Charles V. Gerkin, *The Living Human Document* (Nashville: Abingdon Press, 1984) pp. 39–40, 50.

Bibliography

Theology

Introductory Texts in Narrative Theology

Goldberg, Michael. *Theology and Narrative: A Critical Introduction.* Nashville: Abingdon Press, 1982.

Stroup, George. *The Promise of Narrative Theology: Recovering the Gospel in the Church.* Atlanta: John Knox Press, 1981.

Other Theological and Ethical Texts
Making Significant Use of Narrative Approaches

Allen, Joseph L. *Love and Conflict: A Covenantal Model of Christian Ethics.* Nashville: Abingdon Press, 1984.

Brueggemann, Walter. *The Creative Word: Canon as a Model for Biblical Education.* Philadelphia: Fortress Press, 1982.

————. *The Prophetic Imagination.* Philadelphia: Fortress Press, 1978.

Crossan, John Dominic, *The Dark Interval: Towards a Theology of Story.* Allen, Tex.: Argus Communications, 1975.

————. *In Parables.* New York: Harper & Row, 1973.

Eichrodt, Walther. *Theology of the Old Testament,* vol. 1. The Old Testament Library. Philadelphia: Westminster Press, 1961.

Frei, Hans. *The Eclipse of Biblical Narrative.* New Haven: Yale University Press, 1974.

Gustafson, James M. *Can Ethics Be Christian?* Chicago: University of Chicago Press, 1975.

————. *Treasure in Earthen Vessels.* New York: Harper & Brothers, 1961.

Hauerwas, Stanley. *Character and the Christian Life: A Study in Theological Ethics.* San Antonio: Trinity University Press, 1975.

————. *A Community of Character.* Notre Dame, Ind.: University of Notre Dame Press, 1981.

————. *Vision and Virtue: Essays in Christian Ethical Reflection.* Notre Dame, Ind.: Fides Publishers, 1974.

Hillers, Delbert R. *Covenant: The History of a Biblical Idea*. Baltimore: Johns Hopkins Press, 1969.

Lindbeck, George A. *The Nature of Doctrine: Religion and Theology in a Postliberal Age*. Philadelphia: Westminster Press, 1984.

MacIntyre, Alasdair. *After Virtue*. Notre Dame, Ind.: University of Notre Dame Press, 1981.

McFague, Sallie, *Metaphorical Theology: Models of God in Religious Language*. Philadelphia: Fortress Press, 1982.

———. *Speaking in Parables: A Study in Metaphor and Theology*. Philadelphia: Fortress Press, 1975.

Metz, Johann Baptist. *Faith in History and Society: Toward a Practical Fundamental Theology*. New York: Seabury Press, 1980.

Moltmann, Jürgen. *The Church in the Power of the Spirit*. New York: Harper & Row, 1977.

———. *The Crucified God*. New York: Harper & Row, 1974.

———. *The Trinity and the Kingdom*. San Francisco: Harper & Row, 1981.

Niebuhr, H. Richard. *The Meaning of Revelation*. New York: Macmillan Co., 1941.

———. *The Responsible Self*. New York: Harper & Row, 1963.

Ogletree, Thomas W. *Hospitality to the Stranger*. Philadelphia: Fortress Press, 1985.

Price, Reynolds. *A Palpable God*. New York: Atheneum Publishers, 1978.

Tracy, David, *The Analogical Imagination*. New York: Seabury Press, 1978.

———. *The Blessed Rage for Order*. New York: Seabury Press, Crossroad Book, 1975.

Van Buren, Paul. *The Burden of Freedom: Americans and the God of Israel*. New York: Seabury Press, 1976.

———. *Discerning the Way*. New York: Seabury Press, 1980.

Wood, Charles M. *The Formation of Christian Understanding: An Essay in Theological Hermeneutics*. Philadelphia: Westminster Press, 1981.

Other Important Theological Works
Pertinent to the Perspective of This Book

Heschel, Abraham. *The Prophets*. New York: Harper & Row, Harper Torchbooks; vol. 1, 1969; vol. 2, 1975.

Metz, Johann Baptist. *Faith in History and Society: Toward a Practical Fundamental Theology*. New York: Seabury Press, 1980.

Pannenberg, Wolfhart. *Anthropology in Theological Perspective*. Philadelphia: Westminster Press, 1985.

———. *Theology and the Kingdom of God*. Philadelphia: Westminster Press, 1969.

———. *The Idea of God and Human Freedom*. Philadelphia: Westminster Press, 1973.

Literary Critical Studies of Narrative

Crites, Stephen. "The Narrative Quality of Experience." *Journal of the American Academy of Religion*, 1971, pp. 290–307.

Frye, Northrop. *Anatomy of Criticism*. Princeton, N.J.: Princeton University Press, 1957.

———. *The Educated Imagination*. Bloomington, Ind.: Indiana University Press, 1964.

———. *Fables of Identity: Studies in Poetic Mythology*. New York: Harcourt, Brace and World, 1963.

———. *The Great Code: The Bible and Literature*. New York: Harcourt Brace Javonovich, 1982.

Kermode, Frank. *The Genesis of Secrecy: On the Interpretation of Narrative*. Cambridge, Mass.: Harvard University Press, 1979.

Kort, Wesley A. *Narrative Elements and Religious Meanings*. Philadelphia: Fortress Press, 1975.

Scholes, Robert, and Robert Kellogg. *The Nature of Narrative*. London: Oxford University Press, 1966.

Wicker, Brian. *The Story-shaped World: Fiction and Metaphysics: Some Variations on a Theme*. Notre Dame, Ind.: University of Notre Dame Press, 1975.

Wiggins, James B., ed. *Religion as Story*. New York: Harper & Row, 1975.

Practical Theology, Pastoral Theology, and Pastoral Care

Modern Pastoral Care Classics

Boisen, Anton. *The Exploration of the Inner World*. New York: Harper & Row, 1952.

Clebsch, William A., and Charles R. Jaekle. *Pastoral Care in Historical Perspective*. Englewood Cliffs, N.J.: Prentice-Hall, 1964.

Hiltner, Seward. *Preface to Pastoral Theology*. Nashville: Abingdon Press, 1958.

McNeill, John T. *A History of the Cure of Souls*. New York: Harper & Brothers, 1951.

Recent Books to Be Compared with This Book

Browning, Don S. *The Moral Context of Pastoral Care*. Philadelphia: Westminster Press, 1976.

———. *Religious Ethics and Pastoral Care*. Philadelphia: Fortress Press, 1983.

———, ed. *Practical Theology: The Emerging Field in Theology, Church, and World*. San Francisco: Harper & Row, 1983.

Campbell, Alastair V. *Rediscovering Pastoral Care*. Philadelphia: Westminster Press, 1981.

Capps, Donald, *Biblical Approaches to Pastoral Counseling*. Philadelphia: Westminster Press, 1981.
———. *Pastoral Care and Hermeneutics*. Philadelphia: Fortress Press, 1984.
Gerkin, Charles V. *Crisis Experience in Modern Life: Theory and Theology for Pastoral Care*. Nashville: Abingdon Press, 1979.
———. *The Living Human Document: Re-visioning Pastoral Counseling in a Hermeneutical Mode*. Nashville: Abingdon Press, 1984.
Holifield, E. Brooks. *A History of Pastoral Care in America*. Nashville: Abingdon Press, 1983.
Oglesby, William B. *Biblical Themes for Pastoral Care*. Nashville: Abingdon Press, 1980.
Whitehead, James D., and Evelyn E. Whitehead. *Method in Ministry: Theological Reflection and Christian Ministry*. New York: Seabury Press, 1980.
Winquist, Charles E. *Practical Hermeneutics: A Revised Agenda for Ministry*. Chico, Calif.: Scholars Press, 1981.

Philosophical Hermeneutics

Bauman, Zygmunt. *Hermeneutics and Social Science*. New York: Columbia University Press, 1978.
Fingarette, Herbert. *The Self in Transformation*. New York: Harper & Row, 1965.
Gadamer, Hans-Georg. *Philosophical Hermeneutics*. Berkeley, Calif.: University of California Press, 1976.
———. *Truth and Method*. New York: Seabury Press, 1975.
Habermas, Jürgen. *Knowledge and Human Interests*. Boston: Beacon Press, 1971.
Ihde, Don. *Hermeneutic Phenomenology: The Philosophy of Paul Ricoeur*. Evanston, Ill.: Northwestern University Press, 1971.
Palmer, Richard. *Hermeneutics*. Evanston, Ill.: Northwestern University Press, 1969.
Reagan, Charles E., and David Stewart, eds. *The Philosophy of Paul Ricoeur*. Boston: Beacon Press, 1978.
Ricoeur, Paul. *Essays Biblical Interpretation*. Philadelphia: Fortress Press, 1980.
———. *Freedom and Nature*. Evanston, Ill.: Northwestern University Press, 1966.
———. *Hermeneutics and the Human Sciences*. Cambridge: Cambridge University Press, 1981.
———. *History and Truth*. Evanston, Ill.: Northwestern University Press, 1965.
———. *Interpretation Theory: Discourse and the Surplus of Meaning*. Forth Worth, Tex.: Texas Christian University Press, 1976.
———. *The Rule of Metaphor: Multi-disciplinary Studies of the Creation of Meaning in Language*. Toronto: University of Toronto Press, 1981.
———. *Time and Narrative*, vol. 1. Chicago: University of Chicago Press, 1984.

Spence, Donald P. *Narrative Truth and Historical Truth: Meaning and Interpretation in Psychoanalysis*. New York: W. W. Norton & Co., 1982.

Psychology and Social Science

Bellah, Robert N. *The Broken Covenant: American Civil Religion in a Time of Trial*. New York: Seabury Press, 1975.

————, Richard Madsen, William M. Sullivan, Ann Swidler, and Steven M. Tipton. *Habits of the Heart: Individualism and Commitment in American Life*. Berkeley, Calif.: University of California Press, 1985.

Berger, Peter L. *Facing Up to Modernity*. New York: Basic Books, 1977.

————and Thomas Luckmann. *The Social Construction of Reality*. Garden City, N.Y.: Doubleday & Co., Anchor Books, 1967.

————, Brigette Berger, and Hansfield Kellner. *The Homeless Mind*. New York: Random House, 1973.

Glock, Charles Y., and Robert N. Bellah, eds. *The New Religious Consciousness*. Berkeley, Calif.: University of California Press, 1976.

Greven, Philip. *The Protestant Temperament: Patterns of Child-rearing, Religious Experience, and the Self in Early America*. New York: Alfred A. Knopf, 1978.

Kantor, David, and William Lehr. *Inside the Family*. San Francisco: Jossey-Bass, 1975.

Kohut, Heinz. *The Restoration of the Self*. New York: International Universities Press, 1977.

Lifton, Robert Jay. *The Broken Connection*. New York: Simon & Schuster, 1979.

Marris, Peter. *Loss and Change*. New York: Random House, Pantheon Books, 1974.

Schutz, Alfred, and Thomas Luckmann. *The Structures of the Life-world*. Evanston, Ill.: Northwestern University Press, 1973.

Sennett, Richard. *Authority*. New York: Random House, Vintage Books, 1981.

————. *The Fall of Public Man*. New York: Alfred A. Knopf, 1977.

Vidich, Arthur, and Joseph Bensman. *Small Town in Mass Society: Class, Power and Religion in a Rural Community*. Princeton, N.J.: Princeton University Press, 1958.

Weber, Max. *The Protestant Ethic and the Spirit of Capitalism*. New York: Seabury Press, 1958.

Index